Macalister, Robert Alexander Stewart, 1870-1950.
A century of excavation in Palestine

A Century of Excavation in Palestine

BOOKS ON SIMILAR SUBJECTS

A CENTURY OF EXCAVATION IN THE LAND OF THE PHARAOHS
By James Baikie, F.R.A.S.

EGYPTIAN PAPYRI AND PAPYRUS HUNTING
By James Baikie, F.R.A.S.

BABYLONIAN LIFE AND HISTORY
By Sir Ernest Wallis Budge, Litt.D., F.S.A.

No. 5.

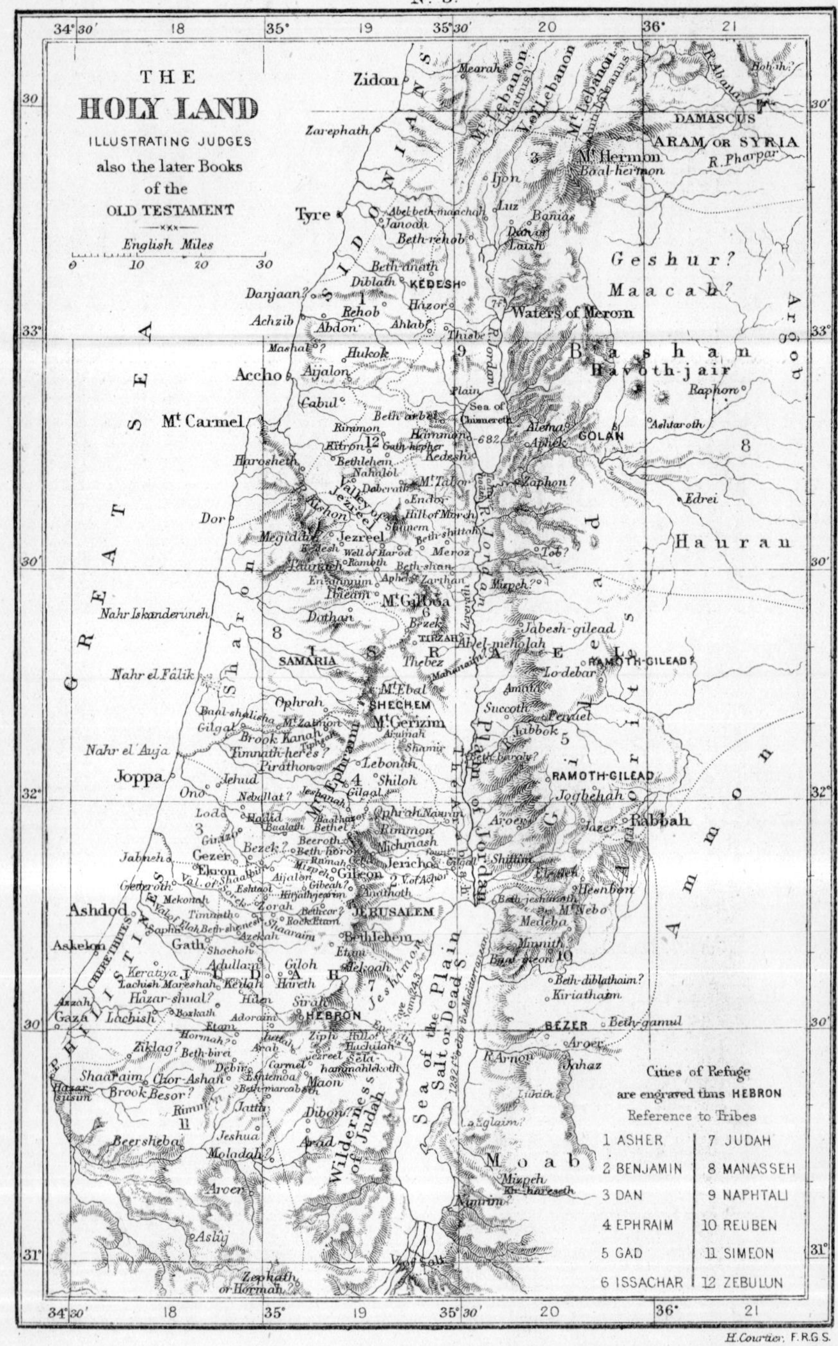

H. Courtier, F.R.G.S.

A Century of Excavation in Palestine

BY

R. A. S. MACALISTER

LL.D., Litt.D., F.S.A.

PROFESSOR OF CELTIC ARCHÆOLOGY, UNIVERSITY COLLEGE, DUBLIN

FORMERLY DIRECTOR OF EXCAVATIONS, PALESTINE EXPLORATION FUND

WITH 36 ILLUSTRATIONS

LONDON

THE RELIGIOUS TRACT SOCIETY

4, Bouverie Street, E.C.4

MADE IN GREAT BRITAIN
PRINTED BY WM. CLOWES AND SONS, LTD., LONDON AND BECCLES.

TO

MY OLD FRIEND

ERNEST W. GURNEY MASTERMAN, M.D.

SOMETIME OF JERUSALEM,

HON. SEC. PALESTINE EXPLORATION FUND

AS A MEMORIAL

OF OUR LONG AND HAPPY FELLOWSHIP

PREFACE

THE purpose of this volume is sufficiently expressed by its title, so that a formal preface is superfluous. An endeavour is here made to present a statement of the knowledge that has been acquired of the history and the civilisation of Palestine, by the researches that have been carried out there during the past hundred years.

The book is not primarily intended for those who have devoted their lives to a special study of Semitics. On this account it has been deemed advisable to spell Hebrew and other Semitic proper names in their popular form, omitting the diacritic signs used to distinguish the peculiar sounds of the Semitic languages. For the same reason, footnote references to authorities have been omitted; but the reader who desires further information as to the various excavations here summarised, will find a short bibliography at the end of the volume.

I have to express my acknowledgments to the Palestine Exploration Fund, for permission to reproduce numerous illustrations from their publications, and for the loan of blocks; to the Rev. Prof. L. B. Paton, of Hartford Theological Seminary, Connecticut, for kindly sending me two photographic prints (Figs. 7 and 10) and for allowing me to make use of them ; to Philadelphia University Museum, for leave to copy the figure of the Beisan stele from their *Museum Journal ;* to the authorities of Harvard University Press, for permission to use two illustrations from the sumptuous memoir on the Samaria excavation ; to M. Paul Geuthner, of Paris, publisher of Weill's *La Cité de David,* for leave to reproduce the illustration of the Theodotos inscription, from that work ; and to the Department of Antiquities, Jerusalem, for the loan of the blocks of the illustrations of the Tell Barak Sarcophagus and the Ascalon bust, from their *Museum Bulletin.*

R. A. S. M.

DUBLIN,

July, 1925.

CONTENTS

LIST OF ILLUSTRATIONS

A CENTURY OF EXCAVATION IN PALESTINE

CHAPTER I

A SKETCH OF THE HISTORY OF EXCAVATION IN PALESTINE

"A CENTURY of Excavation in Palestine." The requirements of uniformity with a companion volume on Egypt impose its title upon this book; but to some extent it is a misnomer. Not more than sixty years have passed since the first attempts were made, in modern times, to find out the secrets hidden in the soil of the Holy Land. We say "in modern times": for it is on record that the pious Empress Helena, in the year A.D. 326, conducted certain excavations in her search for the Holy Sepulchre. But from then onward, until about the middle of the nineteenth century, no excavations took place in Palestine, unless we choose to count those of gold-seekers, pillaging ancient tombs. Throughout the Middle Ages crowds of pilgrims visited the country; but these were content to accept what their guides told them, and made no independent researches of their own. Indeed, they could never have had the opportunity, even had they the mind or the skill to do so.

It is truly fortunate that excavation was so long delayed. Much damage, and little good, would have been done by excavation, at a time when Archæology was still in the rudimentary stage of development in which we find it, so late as the beginning of the nineteenth century. Even as matters stand, the commercial hunt for "curiosities," and for works of ancient art, divorced from their archæological contexts, has done endless and incalculable mischief, in Palestine no less than in other centres of ancient civilisation. The collector, whose sole aim it is to hang trophies on his walls, or to fill the shelves of his cabinets, is one of the greatest of all enemies of science. A painted vase, be it never so artistic, is shorn of half its scientific value if no record has been preserved of the place where it was found, and of any other objects that may have been associated with it, however insignificant these may be. The art of discovering and of interpreting antiquities has had to be developed just like the arts of music or of painting ; until it had been acquired, excavators were working in the dark, and by their operations were unconsciously destroying evidence, the importance of which could be realised only with the growth of scientific knowledge.

Palestine has a uniqueness in the world, as the stage on which were transacted the historical events in the background of the faiths of Judaism and of Christianity. But we must not forget that in addition to this religious significance, the country had no little importance in secular history. It was the land-bridge between sea and desert; the causeway over which ran the great trade-route between Africa and Asia. It was a stage on the caravan road between the Euphrates and the Nile. Across its soil Egypt and Babylon exchanged their wealth and their wares. Here different empires met. Here, if anywhere, we might hope to find overlapping civilisations, teaching us how they influenced one another, and helping us to solve difficult chronological problems by revealing a succession of contemporary cultures.

During the Middle Ages only the religious aspect of Palestine exploration appealed to travellers. Visitors to the country were pilgrims, seeking to be edified by a contemplation of the sites and of the scenes associated with the sacred personages of the Old and New Testaments; more especially those connected with the foundation of the Christian faith. To make such a pilgrimage was an enterprise attended with no small discomfort and risk; little wonder that it was sometimes imposed as a penance upon delinquents. The Muslim natives of the land were jealous and unfriendly; the government authorities were as a rule openly hostile. Pilgrims, in their own interest, were obliged to conform to strict rules of conduct, established for them by the local ecclesiastical authorities. Every step had to be taken under the direction of their monastic hosts. From the moment of their arrival, until their final departure, they were personally conducted from one holy place

travellers come under the protection of powerful resident officers, representing their respective nations. There is thus more opportunity for leisurely study, and in consequence the books produced during these later centuries are much fuller of descriptive material. As favourable examples, selected from the beginning, the middle, and the end of the seventeenth century, we may name the works of the Englishman George Sandys, who visited the country in 1610; and of the two French ecclesiastics Doubdan (1652) and Morison (1697); the last named has given us a narrative of great charm.

But already in the sixteenth century we can perceive the stirring of a purely scientific interest in the country and in its products. The botanists Belon du Mans (1553) and Rauwolff (1582) traverse it; and although such men as these by no means overlooked the religious importance of the country, their eyes were continually open for fresh light on their own special science. Incidentally they noted many curious points relating to the manners and customs of the people, and to other branches of study, not directly connected with religious interests. In a country so rich in remains of antiquity, it is not surprising that these now began to attract attention for their own sake. Onwards from the days of Kootwyck, or Cotovicus as he Latinised himself (1619), we begin to find inscriptions copied, buildings measured and planned, and tomb-chambers explored and described.

As landmarks on the road of archæological

exploration, from this time onwards to 1824, we may name in succession Maundrell (1697), Pococke (1743), Shaw (1757), Seetzen, the discoverer of the ruins of Jerash and Amman (1806–7), Burckhardt, the discoverer of Petra (1810–12), Buckingham (1821), Irby and Mangles (1823). These are just a few selected from the principal contributors to knowledge. The dates given are those of the journeys recorded rather than of the actual publication, which in some cases were considerably later. In 1714 Hadrian Reland, though not himself an explorer of the country, performed the useful service of "taking stock" of the accumulated sum of knowledge. In his *Palæstina ex monumentis veteribus illustrata* he presented a laboriously classified compilation, even yet of great value as a work of reference, of all the topographical facts available in the literature that had appeared down to his time.

The "century" of our title opens in 1824, one hundred years before the day on which the writing of this book was taken in hand. What was known of Palestinian topography and history at that date? For its history, in the times preceding the Captivities, the Old Testament was as yet the only source of information available; for Josephus can hardly be called an independent authority for that period. The mysterious writings of Egypt and of Babylon had already begun to reveal the secrets which they enshrined; but the most important documents relative to Palestinian history were as yet undiscovered. A classification of Palestinian antiquities was quite impossible. Indeed, only a limited number of types of objects was regarded as worthy of serious attention. The value of inscriptions was recognised; but old pots, such as would now be eloquent to an archæologist, were mere curiosities, that might be Jebusite, Hebrew, Roman, or Arab for all their possessors could tell. The general course of the development of civilisation, through the ages of stone, bronze, and iron, was only beginning to be understood. So far as the geographical aspect of the country was concerned, the main facts were already familiar. A traveller knew that when he landed at Jaffa he would find himself on the margin of a wide plain, after crossing which he would have to ascend through tortuous valleys in order to reach Jerusalem. He knew that then, after passing Jerusalem, he would descend, on the other side of the mountainous ridge, into the Jordan valley; but as yet no one was aware of the extraordinary depth below the level of the Mediterranean Sea to which this journey would take him. Throughout the country the sites of the chief towns were known; most of them, such as Jerusalem and Hebron, had never been lost to sight. But the lesser sites of Biblical and secular history had passed into oblivion, and their recovery was a task that had scarcely been begun. The sacred sites of the Gospels had been fixed by traditions of varying ages and varying authenticity—some of them on very slender grounds: the critical spirit of the nineteenth century was yet to open fire upon this cherished inheritance. Certain Greek and Latin inscriptions throughout the country had been copied, with more or less accuracy. Some Semitic inscriptions from Palmyra and elsewhere were also on record, although but little progress had been made in their interpretation. The *tells*, the mounds of accumulation covering the sites of ancient cities and villages, had not escaped occasional notice; but their supreme importance was as yet unimagined. In a word, the available knowledge of what is sometimes uncouthly called "Palestinology" was scrappy and patchy in the last degree: the man destined to set the science upon a firm basis had not yet come forward.

He was, however, biding his time. His name was Edward Robinson; in 1824 he was a teacher of Hebrew in the Theological Seminary of Andover, Massachusetts. From his boyhood he had dreamed of visiting and of travelling in Palestine; and he had devoured all the literature on which he could lay hands, relating to the country. This he classified, much as Reland had done about a hundred years before; and the study impressed upon him the incompleteness of the information available on many important questions. Just at the time which at the moment interests us, he had attained the age of thirty, and he thought it well to seek release from the duties of his post, in order to proceed to Germany, for study under Gesenius and other masters of the day. He had projected a treatise on Biblical Geography; but when he came to write it, he found it impossible to do so satisfactorily, in the imperfect condition of knowledge. He determined, therefore, to realise his early dream and to visit and investigate the country in person, seeking on the spot the answers to questions that none of his books could resolve.

He carried out this design in the year 1838. In April of that year, having travelled from Cairo by way of the Sinaitic Peninsula, he crossed the frontier of Palestine and found himself in Beer-Sheba. He began his journey with very moderate expectations; indeed, with very moderate intentions. But he reaped a harvest of extraordinary richness. For two months he meandered through the country, Bible in hand, following out all the topographical hints which its record supplies, and supplementing his observations with the knowledge acquired from his preliminary study of the literature. Fourteen years later, in 1852, he paid a second visit to the country, of about equal duration, and then made large additions to the material collected on the first journey.

Robinson's interests were strictly limited. He devoted himself almost exclusively to topography, especially to Biblical topography. Archæology for him was only of secondary importance; while upon folk-lore, natural history, and other branches of study, he only casually touches. His chief aim was the identification of Biblical sites: for which he depended mainly upon the conservation of ancient place-names in modern speech. We now know that this is a dangerous basis of argument; such identifications have to be checked by other tests, unsuspected in Robinson's time. There is evidence that place-names were not invariably fixed in the same spot throughout the long course of ages that separate us from the Biblical era : and sometimes an ancient and a modern name, especially when written in European letters, have a superficial resemblance which conceals from the unwary a complete philological incompatibility. Notwithstanding this unavoidable weakness in Robinson's work, nothing can take from him the credit due for having filled the map with scores of names that till then were quite unknown to the world.

Robinson was most fortunate in his travelling companion. As a guide he had secured the services of Eli Smith, for many years a missionary in Syria. A professional dragoman—if there were such persons at all at the time—would have ruined his work. Had he entrusted himself to the tender mercies of one of these gentry, he would have been fleeced right and left, hurried past important places, and distracted with administrative difficulties. Smith was conversant with the language and the psychology of the people of the country; he had a thorough knowledge of the conditions of travel, derived from a long experience ; and he was as enthusiastic in the work as was Robinson himself. While we accord to Robinson the credit which is his by right, we should not forget Eli Smith, whose collaboration made Robinson's work, in such an extraordinarily short space of time, possible ; and whose sharc in it was probably greater than Robinson admits, or than the world has acknowledged.

It was inevitable that Robinson's work should suffer from the defects of his time. He was a pioneer ; and it is seldom given to pioneers to perfect their undertakings. Even when a Paul plants, an Apollos must water. Moreover, he carried with him, from the rigid New-England puritanism of his upbringing, a strong anti-"popery" prejudice ; this, like all other prejudices, inhibits a true balance of judgement whenever it comes into play. Traditional identifications, especially those centreing in the Church of the Holy Sepulchre, he views with a jaundiced eye. To the overpowering historical and architectural interest of the church he is totally blind. He records, apparently without remorse, that he visited the building but once: saw priests, who looked like "scoundrels" performing some "mummery": left the building in disgust, and never entered it again. When he can call anything "monkish," he consigns it without further ado to limbo. Needless to say, such an attitude is just as reprehensibly unscientific as that of the visitor, be he mediæval pilgrim or modern globe-trotter, who swallows at a gulp everything that his guide chooses to tell him.

It must not be supposed that Robinson was the first to question the authenticity of the Church of the Holy Sepulchre. Already in 1639 the ponderous ecclesiastical topographer Quaresmius had felt moved to animadvert on the "western heretics" who threw doubt on the traditions of this site ; and in 1741 Jonas Korte published his *Reise nach dem gelobten*

Lande, which contained a powerful onslaught upon the claims of this Church. But Robinson was the first to popularise a suspicion of the baselessness of these long-treasured traditions. His attack upon them opened the flood-gates, and admitted a rush of controversial printers' ink; most of which might just as well have remained stored in its reservoir, awaiting some purpose less dismally futile.

Robinson's success soon stimulated emulation. He had led the way in two lines of investigation; in surface topography, and in a criticism of tradition. He was the first to reveal the wealth of unsuspected scientific truth awaiting research, even in "the least of all lands." First among his followers may be named Titus Tobler, who had come as a tourist in 1835: this visit aroused his serious interest, and on returning to his German home he proceeded to prepare himself, as Robinson had done, for systematic topographical work. In three later visits he proved himself a worthy follower of his American predecessor; the volumes in which he published the results of his investigations are still valuable. He was especially thorough in studying Jerusalem, to which Robinson's sectarian prejudices had prevented him from giving the full attention that it rightfully demands.

After Tobler, the most important topographer calling for notice is the Frenchman Victor Guérin, who, beginning in 1852, accomplished single-handed the task of mapping Palestine, and of writing a descriptive monograph in seven large volumes, incorporating the notes that he had accumulated. His map was published in 1863. It was preceded, however, by a yet more important work of cartography, the map of C. W. M. Van de Velde, published in 1858. This was the best available map of Palestine until the completion of the Ordnance Survey, under the auspices of the Palestine Exploration Fund.

About the middle of the nineteenth century we reach the era of excavation, as contrasted with surface exploration. In the year 1850, Félicien de Saulcy suffered the loss of his wife. Seeking a distraction in his grief, he made a tour in the Holy Land, in the course of which he persuaded himself that he had found the sites of Sodom and Gomorrah. While he was in Jerusalem his attention was especially attracted by the great series of rock-cut burial-chambers to the north of the city, popularly called "The Tombs of the Kings." This sepulchre, like so many others of its kind, from which it differs only by its superior size, is doubtless the sepulchral vault of some family of wealth and position belonging to the Herodian period : the debased Classical decorations of the sadly-damaged portico prohibit us from assigning it to a date more remote. None of the various attempts that have been made to identify the owners of this great monument is free from difficulty ; this applies even to the theory most generally current, that it is the memorial of Queen Helena of Adiabene, of whose conversion to Judaism, and settlement in Jerusalem, we may read in the pages of Josephus. Contrary to all the architectural evidence, De Saulcy accepted the traditional name as authentic, and saw in this *hypogæum* the actual tombs of the pre-exilic kings of Judah. He even went so far as to determine, to his own satisfaction, where the body of each king had been deposited. Fragments of a sarcophagus-lid, richly decorated with a floral scroll-work ornament, found by him in the sepulchre, he boldly and without any qualification called the cover of David's coffin.

When De Saulcy first visited the sepulchre it was much cumbered with earth. We can picture in what condition it was at the time with the help of old woodcuts, such as those published in Guérin's *La Terre Sainte*, or Thomson's *Land and the Book*. De Saulcy explored it, at his first visit, as well as he could. Even in the eighteen-fifties, however (when identifications of the kind had a better chance of a favourable hearing than they would have now), De Saulcy's theories were received with a not unnatural scepticism, which stimulated in him a desire to examine the chambers more thoroughly. Accordingly he sought and obtained from the Turkish authorities a permit to excavate the sepulchre, a work which he carried out in 1863. He found a number of sarcophagi, which he removed to France; they are now in the Louvre. One of them is inscribed; but the inscription so far from solving the problem, raises a new one. For it names as the owner of the sarcophagus a certain "Queen Sadan" or "Sadah"—the name is written twice, in different forms of the Semitic alphabet, and with this variation in orthography. But recorded history has no light to throw upon the personality of this royal lady.

Our subject is "a century of *excavation* in Palestine;" and although surface topography is of great importance—indeed, some aspects of the results of excavation are merely subordinate to the study of surface topography, as when it is used to test the identification of ancient sites—we must not expend too much space in speaking outside our brief. We shall not linger, therefore, over the work of De Vogüé, or of De Luynes, or of others who have enlarged our knowledge of the face of the country. But there is one publication to which a passing reference must be made, less on account of its own merits, which are exiguous, than of the consequences to which it led. In 1864 Ermete Pierotti, an engineer in the employ of the Turkish authorities in Jerusalem, put forth a work in two pretentious folio volumes called "Jerusalem Explored." His official duties had given him opportunities of entering buildings which for military or religious reasons were taboo to the majority of foreigners. He made good, though not the best possible, use of these privileges; the book is on the whole unsatisfactory, and in many respects is inaccurate. But it was these very defects which led Sir George Grove and his friends to the conclusion that the time had come when something more systematic should be attempted. In the year when Pierotti's work appeared, the preliminary steps were taken that led to the foundation of the Palestine Exploration Fund, the first of the several societies now in existence having for their purpose the collection of materials for study, connected with the Holy Land.

The public meeting at which the new society was constituted took place in June, 1865, under the presidency of the Archbishop of York. Many distinguished people attended the meeting, which seems to have been marked with great enthusiasm. The following guiding principles were laid down at the time ; and they have been recognised as fundamental ever since, by those responsible for the conduct of the society. The work was to be conducted on strictly scientific principles. The society was to collect facts in every relevant department of knowledge. It was to abstain from controversy, taking no corporate responsibility for such theories of its officers and of others as might appear from time to time in its publications. Further, although, from the first, one of its leading aims would be to contribute to the elucidation of Biblical problems, it was definitely not to be a religious society, committed to any form of dogma. Many diverse creeds and forms of belief are represented among its supporters.

Shortly after the meeting above referred to, a prospectus was issued, with the purpose of attracting subscribers. A preliminary programme of the contemplated work was there set forth. In *Archæology* special mention was made, as was natural, of Jerusalem, and of the problems relating to the Holy Places and their identification, which had become insistent since the iconoclastic work of Robinson. Just at the time an elaborate survey of Jerusalem was in progress, on behalf of the Baroness Burdett-Coutts, who had hoped to have the privilege of installing a proper water-supply in the city. This survey was being conducted by Captain (afterwards General Sir Charles) Wilson; and it was expected to put at the disposal of every one a full knowledge of what was to be seen above ground—an expectation which it amply fulfilled. But practically nothing was as yet known of what lay hidden beneath the surface. Besides Jerusalem, the prospectus mentioned a number of other places throughout the country as promising sites for exploration—Shechem, Caesarea, Gilgal, Jericho, Beth-Shean, Jezreel. Looking back from the standpoint of knowledge that has accumulated since, mainly through the labours of the Fund itself, it is curious to find Guérin's absurd identification of the Tomb of Joshua mentioned among these important sites as a promising digging centre.

Topography (including a detailed survey of the whole country), *Geology*, *Botany*, *Zoology*, and *Meteorology* were also indicated as sciences that could be enriched by the researches of the society. It is not within the scope of the present work to review the contributions to these departments of knowledge that have thus been made; we may pass them by with a bare acknowledgment. We need not say very much even about the great Survey of Palestine, conducted on behalf of the Fund by Lieuts. Conder and Kitchener (afterwards Lord Kitchener of Khartoum). This almost monopolised the society's activities for many years. It resulted in the publication of a map of the country, to a scale of one inch to one mile, accompanied with a series of large volumes of memoirs on Topography, Place-names, and Fauna and Flora, and a special volume on Jerusalem.

The Survey was not, however, the first undertaking of the newly-founded society. The claims of Jerusalem for special attention were too insistent to be disregarded ; with the exuberance of enthusiastic youth, the society boldly tackled some of its obscurest problems. It is easy—and proverbially futile—to be wise after the event. While we recognise this, we must yet permit ourselves to describe the premature assault on Jerusalem as a fundamental mistake. One of the many minor sites in the country should have been attacked first, and worked out thoroughly, in order to learn the general character and chronology of the antiquities of the country Excavation is necessarily destructive. Facts are torn from the ground, to be transferred to the explorer's note-book. If not so transferred they are lost for ever. If the excavator has not sufficient knowledge to interpret the facts, their value is proportionally diminished. In 1867 nothing was known about the development of pottery in the country, which is now recognised as being the chief clue to the dating of Palestinian sites and strata. Without potsherds, there is little or nothing to discriminate between a wall of 100 B.C. and a wall of 2000 B.C. : there is marvellously little difference in the masonry. A site of the first importance, such as Jerusalem, ought therefore have been left alone, until the excavators had learnt their business on the *corpus vile* of some place less important, the destruction of which would have involved less serious loss.

A further mistake was made in the instructions that were issued to Lieut. Warren (afterwards Sir Charles Warren), who had been selected to carry out the work at Jerusalem. It was expected that the projected excavations would settle, once for all, the controversies regarding the Holy Places. A programme sufficient for several lifetimes was laid before the man who was to work for three years. It is almost pathetic to look back to those early days, and to read of the eager hopes that problems of this nature would be solved by the expenditure of a few hundreds of pounds, and the turning over of some spadefuls of earth. But the essential mistake lay not so much in the magnitude of these expectations, as in the drawing up of a definitely conceived programme, of whatever nature. A true excavator will attack his chosen site with but one intention--to find out what it contains. Few questions are more irritating, and more unanswerable, than the stock inquiry which any excavator may expect to be asked by any casual tourist who happens to pay him a visit—" What do you expect to find ? " An obsession as to what ought to be in a site will blind the excavator as to what actually is there. In his disappointment at unrealised hopes, he is apt to forget the gifts, often rich enough, that the gods actually send him. We can give a striking illustration of this principle from Ireland. Certain worthy folk got it into their heads that the Israelite Ark of the Covenant lay hidden under one of the mounds on Tara Hill, where, they professed to believe, it had been concealed by the prophet Jeremiah. We shall leave to the reader the pleasure of making the comments appropriate to a theory of this kind, and merely record the facts of the case. In the pursuit of this chimaera they dug up and destroyed the mound. They did not find the Ark, but, it is understood, they did find certain objects or structures which would have been of value for local history. Not being interested in local history, they paid no heed to them, and these were lost. It is almost a universal experience that an excavation will mock the hopes that are entertained of it, while at the same time it will give the excavator rewards of which he never dreamed, if only he is prepared to receive them.

Warren's work at Jerusalem was carried out mainly by tunnelling—the most unsatisfactory of all excavation processes. Vertical shafts were dug to a certain depth, after which horizontal galleries were driven through the soil in the required direction. Sometimes this method of working is inevitable. A cantankerous or greedy landowner, a building that must not be removed, a cemetery still in use—all these are obstacles that cannot be surmounted, and must therefore be circumvented by some such means. But only under compulsion of the kind is tunnelling justifiable. It is very costly work; it is also slow, as the labour of carrying the waste soil through the ever-lengthening gallery cannot be hurried. Moreover, it is very dangerous. The workmen are liable to risks from foul air, from the running of gravel or other unstable material, or from a collapse of the gallery roof. The necessary strutting of the gallery is very expensive. The supervision of workmen is next to impossible ; a man digging at the inner extremity of a narrow tunnel could conceal within his garments an object of obvious value, with but little fear of being detected in the act by his foreman, however vigilant the latter might be. In any case the chance of finding antiquities is reduced to a minimum, as only a very small portion of the soil is touched ; and the superposition of chronological strata cannot be studied at all.

When a building is struck, only a very small portion of its wall is exposed ; not enough to reveal its nature. If it cannot be laid bare, it has to be explored by means of an elaborate network of tunnels, most difficult to plan accurately, and almost sure to miss minor details of the design. Work of this kind is *possible*, as was triumphantly proved long afterwards, when Bliss and Dickie revealed and planned the church of Eudoxia at the Pool of Siloam by this process alone ; but it is never so satisfactory as when the whole building can be exposed, so that all the mutual relations of its parts can be seen at a single *coup d'œil*.

The most important division of Warren's work lay in and around the *Haram esh-Sherif*, the great Muslim shrine which is admitted by all to occupy the site of Solomon's Temple.

His excavations here proved that the immense outer walls, imposing though they be, are in reality far greater than their general appearance would lead the passer-by to suspect; for their base is covered with accumulated rubbish to a depth of from 80 to 120 feet. The aspect of the deep shaft and gallery by which Warren laid bare the foundation of that mighty wall is familiar to all subscribers to the Palestine Exploration Fund, as a diagram of them forms the device on the cover of its periodical *Quarterly Statement*.

Close to these foundations, in a crevice of the rock, Warren found a small vessel of pottery. Had the preliminary excavation of some minor *tell*, suggested above, been carried out, this would have been recognised as being a very commonplace specimen of late Hebrew ware; but as a first discovery, and in view of the romantic situation in which it came to light, it attracted great attention at the time. In all probability it was nothing more important than the receptacle in which a workman had brought olive-oil for the seasoning of his midday meal, and which by some oversight he had forgotten when he returned to his home in the evening.

Another discovery made at this place, which caused great excitement, was a group of marks painted on a foundation stone of the south-east corner of the great wall. These were supposed to be Phœnician characters, and to come from the hand of one of King Hiram's labourers. But although some of them—not all—superficially resemble Phœnician or Old Hebrew characters, no one has ever succeeded in grouping them together, much less in making translateable words of them. Probably they were mere graffiti, with no special significance.

Similar tunnels were driven under the accumulation in the Tyropoeon valley, close to Robinson's Arch. Robinson's Arch is the spring of a colossal archway, which breaks out from the western wall of the Haram area, close to its southern corner. When Robinson inspected it, he did not at first recognise its nature. He took it for building-stones that had been thrown out of place by an earthquake. But a chance remark by one of his Jerusalem friends, an American missionary named Whiting, that the stones looked like part of a large arch, put him on the track of identifying it with the viaduct which, according to Josephus, ran from the Temple to the Xystus or colonnade built by Herod. This explanation was verified by Warren. The foundations of piers were discovered, in a line with the existing fragment, showing that the causeway had been supported on a series of arches. It was proved, moreover, that this had not been the first viaduct over the Tyropoeon at this place ; for a voussoir cut to a different radius lay at the bottom of the 75 feet of accumulation that here cumbered the valley. This stone must necessarily have belonged to an older structure of a similar nature : presumably the bridge broken down (as we learn from Josephus) at the time of Pompey's invasion. The old water-course running along the floor of the valley was laid bare ; and here and

" ROYAL STAMP " OF HEBRON, ON A JAR-HANDLE ; AND THE SEAL OF " SHEMA SERVANT OF JEROBOAM," FOUND AT MEGIDDO.

elsewhere over the whole area of the city and its environs, a number of rock-levels was determined, from which the contour of the site could be drawn with an accuracy never before attainable.

Warren further examined the reservoir called *Birket Israin*, "The Pool of Israel," a large reservoir north of the Haram; one of the competitors for the honour of identification with the Pool of Bethesda. He also began the investigations that, at the moment of writing, after nearly sixty years, are still in progress, for determining the course of the city's ancient walls. One of his most sensational finds was the cutting now appropriately called "Warren's Shaft," the tunnel whereby the ancient Jebusites procured water. A description of this remarkable work will be more suitably postponed to a later page of this book.

The harvest of portable antiquities from Warren's excavation was very small; no doubt in consequence of the use of tunnels. Most interesting were the first two of the jar-handles bearing the so-called "royal stamps," which have now become a stock item in the yield of a Palestinian excavation. These are the handles of rather large, coarsely made jars, usually in a dark reddish or drab ware, upon which is stamped the impression of an oval seal, with a maximum diameter about equal to that of a penny. On the seal is the figure of a flying creature, sometimes a scarabæus with four wings, sometimes a bird with two; in all cases the drawing of this figure is very crude. Above the figure is the Hebrew word *lammelek*, "for the king";

below it is one of the four words, Hebron, Ziph, Socho, Mimshat—the first being at least similar to well-known names of towns, the fourth a word nowhere else found. These stamps present an enigma about which there have been no little controversy, in the pages of the Palestine Exploration Fund's *Quarterly Statement* and elsewhere. It can hardly be said that the questions which they raise have been completely answered. This illustrates how the work of excavation is necessarily endless; for though each undertaking settles a question or two, it raises in its turn a crop of new problems, that otherwise would never have been thought of.

Warren accomplished his work in the face of many difficulties. Most of the local authorities were actively unfriendly; property owners were unsympathetic and extortionate; the remittances from home seem to have arrived very irregularly. After sixty years of experience we can see how unreasonable it was to expect a solution of the labyrinthine problems of Jerusalem topography by making soundings in a number of disconnected places in and around the city. Warren left those problems much where he found them. But he showed how many entirely new and unsuspected treasures were hidden in and around the city, waiting to reward a well-equipped expedition that would attack the site systematically, and with adequate funds.

After the close of Warren's work at Jerusalem, the Palestine Exploration Fund ceased for a time from the work of excavation on a large scale. A few small undertakings of the kind were carried out by Clermont-Ganneau and others—clearances of specific buildings or of tomb-chambers, or exposure of buried portions of walls. The attention of the Fund as a body was absorbed by the task of surveying Western Palestine, and by all the subsidiary work ancillary thereto. For the twenty years which followed the close of Warren's excavation (April, 1870) the record of excavation in Palestine is practically a blank.

The Survey of Palestine called fresh attention to the *tells* scattered through the country. These mounds of accumulation cover and mark the sites of the ancient cities and villages. The word *tell* (the proper plural of which is *talul*) denotes a rounded, usually flat-topped hillock, with straight sloping sides. The formation of such a mound may thus be explained. For the greater part, the cities of the ancient East were built of undressed blocks of stone, set in a mud mortar. The roofs were flat, and were also composed of mud, like the roofs of houses in the modern country villages. When houses thus flimsily constructed chanced to fall, the stones were picked out of the heap of ruin for re-use, and the mud was trampled down to form the subsoil of the new building. Thus a heap of accumulated foundations gradually rose, one over the other, each associated with the pot-sherds and the other antiquities peculiar to its time. The streets also gradually raised their level; for rubbish was allowed to collect, undisturbed by a scavenger, and year after year fresh material was thus added to the pile. For purposes of defence the cities were as a rule constructed on the hill-tops. Not until the period of Roman domination made internal hostility impossible, and held foreign enemies at bay, did the inhabitants venture to leave the cramped areas within their city walls, and to build more open dwelling-places, close to the local source of water. Before this migration took place, the level of the city site had risen to such an extent that whereas the first inhabitants had settled on the natural summit of the hill, the last inhabitants might have been established some thirty or forty feet higher. After the migration, all the stones visible above the surface of the mound were removed for building elsewhere. Nothing was left but what was underground. Wind and rain played on the site, and smoothed down its sides ; but the concealed foundations of the great city wall acted as a revetment, which prevented erosion. This accounts for the flat top which is one of the most characteristic and unmistakable marks of a mound of artificial accumulation in Palestine.

Differing in character from a *tell* is a *khirbeh* or " ruin," although the difference is not always strictly preserved in local terminology. A *khirbeh*, as a rule, is a site on which there are traces of ancient occupation, but no great accumulation of debris. Usually it consists of a cluster of ruined houses, within the area of which the rock often crops to the surface. It is frequently possible to make a plan of a khirbeh with little or no excavation, although modern builders are quite remorseless in despoiling them of their building-stones. Palestine is

THE EXCAVATION OF A "TELL" IN PROGRESS—SHOWING THE FOUNDATIONS OF HOUSE-WALLS.

emphatically not one of the few countries in which there is a healthy public opinion in favour of the protection of ancient buildings ; though a Palestinian might very fairly retort with a reminder of the restrictions prudent for dwellers in glass houses, in view of the wholesale destruction of London city churches, at the *fiat* of the goddess Mammon.

Here and there, within the area of a khirbeh, yawns the mouth of a cistern—a trap for the unwary ; no little precaution is needed in exploring one of these sites. In most cases the buildings of which we can trace the remains are of little interest ; but sometimes meagre relics of a more important structure are to be found—a church, perhaps, or an assembly-hall of some sort. The potsherds, such as besprinkle all ancient sites in Palestine, usually prove that a khirbeh belongs to a late date, Roman, Byzantine, or early Arab ; this date may often be confirmed by the evidence of coins, which are frequently to be picked up, especially after a heavy rain.

If we visit a tell, we are not unlikely to find in its immediate neighbourhood a khirbeh. And it often happens that the khirbeh bears the ancient Biblical name, while the tell is called by some commonplace descriptive name in modern Arabic. The explanation of this seeming anomaly is perfectly simple. The ancient population remained on the tell, the original site, until the comparative peace that they owed to the hated Roman yoke made it possible for them to settle on the more convenient site of the khirbeh. They carried their old name to their new home, and the derelict tell had to be renamed. Usually the last occupation that has left its traces on the tell belongs to the time just preceding the coming of the Romans.

Accordingly, if we open a clearance in the summit of a tell, we shall most probably uncover first a stratum of foundations, associated with pottery and coins which teach us that the houses that stood on this level were built during the stirring times when Antiochus and the Maccabees were fighting on earth the battle of Zeus and Yahweh. We expose the foundations completely, plan the walls, and remove them. Immediately underneath, new foundations will begin to make their appearance. The pottery associated with these will be ruder, not being baked to so hard a consistency ; it will not give the musical clink that we have learnt to associate with pottery of the Maccabean period. Perhaps a few of the " Royal Stamps " will now appear on the jar-handles. Coins will disappear. We are working in, or about, the period of Persian domination. When its remains in their turn have been cleared, and we descend a foot or two deeper, we shall find ourselves in the city of Hezekiah, of Jehoshaphat, or of Solomon : and we shall see a vivid picture of the civilisation, or rather of the non-civilisation, out of the heart of which the ancient prophets arose, to revolutionise man's knowledge of his Maker. Lower down still, we reach the dark days of the Judges ; lower still, the time when the Amorite was filling up the measure of his iniquities. With luck, we may find a tablet or two, written at the time when the kings of the cities of Canaan were petitioning for the help, that never came, against the raiding Aramaeans. At last we come to the rocky core of the hill, on which man first pitched his moving tent close on five thousand years ago. Even then our task is not fully accomplished ; for we are more than likely to find a cave in the limestone, natural or artificial, which served as a dwelling or a burial place for some of the most ancient inhabitants.

Such is the structure of a Palestinian tell. It is difficult to say how many of these mounds exist in the country ; probably at least a couple of hundred. We are now to speak of the few that have been partially excavated, and of the results of this work.

In March, 1890, Dr. (now Sir) Flinders Petrie made his way to Palestine on behalf of the Palestine Exploration Fund to examine the interior of a tell for the first time. The chosen centre of operations was Tell el-Hesy near Gaza ; or, to speak with a more strict accuracy, it was the ancient city of Lachish. Lachish had been identified, on the basis of similarity of name, with a site called Umm Lakis ; but this proved on examination to be a mere late khirbeh, of little importance. The conspicuous mound called Tell el-Hesy rose in the neighbourhood, and at once attracted Petrie's notice : he transferred his attention to it without delay.

Petrie was unquestionably the man fitted above all others to be a pioneer in this branch of investigation. His experience in Egypt had given him an appreciation of the worth of unconsidered trifles such as potsherds, and of small commonplace objects which an excavator who should seek merely for inscriptions or for works of art would be inclined to throw contemptuously aside as impertinences. Petrie has taught us that potsherds have a higher average value even than inscriptions. An inscription tells us nothing but what its author chooses. It is not infrequently unintelligible to us, by reason of its allusions to events or to persons of which we know nothing. It is often meagre; often wilfully misleading. But potsherds never fail of their message, on account of the peculiar nature of pottery. It is easily made, of easily procurable materials; it is therefore cheap. Every household in a community was therefore fully supplied with earthen vessels. Further, it is brittle; no vessel can be kept for very long; sooner or later it is sure to be broken. A broken pot cannot be mended—a fact from which the prophet Jeremiah drew an impressive lesson—and a pot once broken was thrown out as useless. But though broken, its texture is indestructible. The smallest particle of pottery is recognisable for what it is. Broken sherds therefore accumulate in and around every city in huge quantities. Being commercially worthless they are not removed by marauders; they remain where they have fallen, to teach the lesson which they have to convey to the archæologist who digs them up.

Each generation has to make its own pottery; and each generation develops its own style. In texture, shape, and ornament the pottery of one century differs from that of another. The determination of this fact, and the manner of its application, we owe to Prof. Petrie. In a brilliant six weeks' reconnaissance of Tell el-Hesy he laid the foundation of the study of Palestinian ceramics, and his successors have but followed where he has led.

For work of this kind, Petrie was fortunate in his site. One side of the mound had been eroded by a stream. In consequence of this happy chance, the edges of the successive strata were exposed. The excavator did not need to wait patiently for the removal of one layer before he could find what was hidden in the next; he could move up and down the hill at his pleasure, trowel in hand, and pick out and compare potsherds from different levels at once.

On the other hand, it must be admitted that very little, except potsherds, was found, during Petrie's excavation. A few weights, and some fragments of bronze and of iron, are recorded in his report on his work. We now know that Palestine was always a land of comparatively low material culture; its villagers were mere *fellahin*; and very extensive clearances in its tells are necessary before we can hope to find anything more than the commonplace appliances of the daily life of such people. In such a country, an explorer, working for only six weeks, could hardly expect to reap a rich harvest, except by some altogether exceptional and wonderful luck. But Petrie's successor in the service of the Fund, Dr. F. J. Bliss, who was on the site for the greater part of two years, had the like experience. As we turn the pages of his book we can see only too clearly "the nakedness of the land." A considerable number of potsherds with potters' marks—mere meaningless strokes and simple geometrical figures; a collection of bronze tools; much pottery of various periods, some of it painted with rude ornament; a handful of scarabs, useful as aids to the chronological discrimination of the strata; arrowheads, stone objects, and miscellaneous domestic utensils—these are the chief objects that catch the eye. The most important find was a single tablet, with a cuneiform inscription; the first of its kind to be found in the Holy Land. Chronologically it belongs to the Tell el-Amarna series. Its contents, so far as they are intelligible, are intrinsically unimportant; the one fact of significance is its mention of a certain Zimrida, whom we know from one of the Tell el-Amarna letters to have been governor of Lachish. This tablet therefore affords corroboration of the identification of Tell el-Hesy with that ancient city, an identification already made by Dr. Petrie on other grounds.

When the Turkish permit for the excavation of Tell el-Hesy expired, one-third of the mound had been dug down to the rock. The remaining two-thirds still await the excavator. But the excavation showed once for all what the explorer in Palestine may expect. While he need not despair of finding exotic works of art, sometimes of high rank, and also inscriptions of interest, he cannot look for evidences of a native civilisation. All the subsequent excavations have only confirmed this conclusion.

When the work closed finally at Tell el-Hesy, the Palestine Exploration Fund once more turned its attention to Jerusalem, and Bliss was commissioned to take up the work that Warren had dropped a quarter of a century before. In this new undertaking he was happily associated with an excellent draughtsman, Mr. Archibald C. Dickie, now Professor of Architecture at Manchester University.

Bliss found that many difficulties were in store for him ; difficulties which he generously minimises in his memoir on the new excavations at Jerusalem. Such difficulties are inseparable from work of the kind in the neighbourhood of the Holy City. The owners of the land where the chief results are to be expected are inhabitants of the village of Silwan, a place which bears the name, though it is not on the site, of the Biblical Siloam. Bishop Heber wrote a sentimental hymn about " cool Siloam's shady rill " ; but he who has had dealings with that noisome place would gladly see this hymn expunged from our hymn-books, and relegated to the Tophet of oblivion prepared for such futilities. The excavator who would work on the land of a dweller in Silwan must expect to be confronted almost daily with some new annoyance, carefully schemed out in order to increase the exorbitant fee—blackmail rather than rent—which has already passed from his scanty funds into his landlord's pocket.

Much of Bliss's work had to be conducted by

means of tunnels, in order not to disturb the crops on the surface of the ground, for which otherwise compensation of about ten times their value would have had to be paid. But in escaping thus from the Scylla of extortion, the explorer falls into the Charybdis of ecclesiastical suspicion. The curators of the *Haram esh-Sherif* are nervously doubtful of the intentions of Europeans. They cannot believe in an expensive undertaking being carried out for no other purpose than to increase knowledge. The digger either must be hunting for treasure, or must have some nefarious design on the sacred mosque. Even if an explorer start a tunnel half a mile away, driven in a direction contrary to that of the sanctuary, they can be easily persuaded by some interested party that he proposes to accomplish the difficult feat of doubling on his track so soon as he is out of sight, so as to penetrate under the sanctuary, and blow it up.

This will show the kind of troubles that were in store for Bliss. Negotiations about the rent of land and the price of crops were countless and interminable. On one occasion, on some such suspicion as is indicated in the last paragraph, soldiers came down to his works and arrested all his labourers. Another serious obstacle to work in Jerusalem is, and must ever be, the idle curiosity of visitors. It goes without saying that there are residents in the city whose arrival on the scene is always welcome ; it is not of these that I am speaking. It is of others who, especially during the tourist season, come down in droves at all times of the day, and expect the explorer, however busy he may be with administrative or other work, to act as showman; in most cases a mere waste of time.

The results of Bliss's work will be analysed on a later page, as fully as our space will permit. For the present let it suffice to say that he started from the great rock-scarp at the south end of the western ridge of the site of Jerusalem—the traditional Zion—and followed thence a city wall, or rather a complex of city walls, running down the northern side of the Valley of Hinnom, crossing the mouth of the Tyropoeon Valley, and ending at the Pool of Siloam. The foundations of gates and of towers were traced and mapped, and thus the whole of the southern limit of the city, at the time of its greatest extension, was finally determined.

At the Pool of Siloam itself were discovered the foundations of an architecturally very interesting church, built over this sacred site by the Empress Eudoxia. The foundations of another church, of the Byzantine period, with a very beautiful mosaic pavement, came to light on the Mount of Olives, while Bliss was at work, and he was enabled to put it also on record. The difficulties above referred to were probably the cause that no large clearances were made anywhere within the area included by the walls; all exploration here was done by soundings and tunnels. Sections of paved streets, and of drains and aqueducts were discovered in this way, as well as a number of mosaic floors of dwelling-houses, all belonging to the later periods of the

D

We learn by experience ; and experience in the campaign thus inaugurated has taught us the undesirability of this kind of roving commission. It was another illustration of the old mistake of embarking on excavation work with a fixed programme. The programme set before the excavator was, " Find Gath." It would have been better to have said " Excavate Tell es-Safi, and see what it has to tell us, whether you succeed in discovering its ancient name or not." It would have been better to have concentrated on one of these sites, even though it were the most insignificant of the nine—even though the chance of discovering Gath were thereby forfeited—and to have exhausted all its possibilities, than to do what was the only practicable thing in the circumstances, having regard to the short time for which the Turkish permits were issued. Only two years, with a possibility of an extension for a third year, were allowed ; in so brief a space nothing could be done but to make a number of soundings on some of the selected sites.

Excavation by soundings is only a degree less unsatisfactory than excavation by tunnelling. It gives us a little more direct information as to the chronological stratification of the debris ; but not so completely as a large clearance. Preliminary soundings are sometimes justified on the ground that they show whether a site is worth digging or not. But in the first place, they do nothing of the kind ; especially in Palestine, where good " finds " are few and are widely scattered, the chances of discovering anything encouraging in a small sounding are extremely minute. In the second place, an excavator who realises that his work has for its objective knowledge and not loot, will not inquire whether any site is worth digging. *All* sites are worth digging; for although all of them may not enrich a museum, all have *some* new fact to teach us. I have no doubt that Tahutmes III, at Megiddo, indicated to his followers the houses of the principal inhabitants as being especially worth digging, inasmuch as they were the most likely to contain loot; but Tahutmes III, many though his virtues may have been, was not the best of models for a scientific excavator of the twentieth century to imitate. If an explorer has merely dug soundings in a site, he will never know that he is not leaving behind its greatest prize, buried in some part of the mound that he has not explored. He will not have exposed more than fragments of buildings, impossible to explain fully for want of knowledge of their continuation underground. And by leaving the soil cut up in patches he makes the work of the successor, who is to come after him to complete his task, all the more difficult.

Almost any one of the nine sites would have supplied ample material for the two years of the permit. Tell es-Safi alone, in spite of the serious obstacles which it presents, would have taken much longer to excavate properly. Of the nine sites, eight were ultimately granted, after the long delays inseparable from negotiations with the Turkish Government. The ninth site, which was specifically excluded, was the least important of them all. It was an insignificant Roman ruin called Khirbet Askalan; from the way in which the Turkish authorities spoke of it, it was obvious that they had confused it with the city of Ascalon, some twenty miles away.

The conditions under which Turkish permits were issued were based on the sound principle—in which a more civilised government would not do amiss to imitate the Turkish model—that national monuments must not be removed from the country. The excavator had full scientific rights over his finds, so far as copying, illustrating, and publishing were concerned; but their possession must remain with the people of the country whose they are. A commissioner of the Government had to encamp with the excavator, to receive, on behalf of the Government, the whole yield of the excavation, so soon as the excavator had made all the necessary observations and records; and to transmit them to the Imperial Museum at Constantinople.

Of the eight sites left, after the exclusion of Khirbet Askalan, it was not possible to dig in more than four, and that incompletely. These four sites are known by the modern names Tell Zakariya, Tell es-Safi, Tell el-Judeideh, and Tell Sandahannah; not one of which conveys a hint as to the name of the ancient town which it represents.

Tell Zakariya derives its name from the adjoining village of Zakariya, itself apparently called after a holy man, whose name would appear to suggest that he was a Hebrew prophet transformed to a Muslim saint. The mound is not very large; it is roughly triangular in shape, about 1000 feet in length and 500 feet in maximum breadth. It has a most imposing

TELL ZAKARIYA.

appearance as it stands at an angle of the Wady es-Sunt, a valley which doubtless is the same as that called the Valley of Elah in the Old Testament. This was the scene of the picturesque combat between David and Goliath. Through the centre of the valley there runs the almost always dry bed of a stream, the floor of which is covered with just such small rounded water-worn pebbles as would have served the purpose of an expert slinger.

Nothing directly bearing on the identification of Tell Zakariya was revealed by the excavation. But there is every probability that it represents the ancient Azekah. Little is recorded of Azekah in the Old Testament. It appears as a note of place in the story of David and Goliath ; the duel took place " between Socoh and Azekah." The name of Socoh, if not the site, is certainly preserved by a village called Shweikeh, on the opposite side of the valley, and visible from the summit of Tell Zakariya.

Three towers, found close together at the edge of the mound to the west, indicated that there had been a wall surrounding the city. This was not traced, however, owing to shortness of time. Most of the work was concentrated on an inner citadel or acropolis, which was wholly contained within the area, at its southern end, and was surrounded with a strong wall of its own, fortified with eight large towers. Such an inner citadel was probably a feature of most Palestinian cities, although this example at Tell Zakariya is the best that has yet been found. Its purpose obviously was to give a second line of defence to the inhabitants, in case of the outer wall being breached by a besieging enemy. The technical name for a stronghold of this kind, in Hebrew, was *metsudah*. Not improbably the citadel at Tell Zakariya was primarily the work of Rehoboam, who, as the Chronicler informs us (II Chron. xi 9), fortified Azekah along with a number of other cities. There was, however, evidence that it had been repaired or enlarged at a later date.

Inside the citadel the area was filled with what were little better than flimsy huts, differing in no respect from those that were found in a clearance in the middle of the city, outside the citadel. Except for one small jar containing a number of Egyptian beads and scarabs, the latter bearing the names of Tahutmes III and of Amenhotep III, the yield of the tell was comparatively scanty. The experience of Tell el-Hesy was repeated ; the excavator was working in the remains of a people of low culture, entirely dependent upon Egypt and the Aegean, to a lesser degree on the empires of Mesopotamia, for its arts and its civilisation.

Some remarkable cisterns and rock-cuttings were observed on the sides of the hill, notably one very large cave, entirely artificial, consisting of a labyrinth of about forty chambers, large and small, united by doorways, roof-openings, and connecting passages.

Tell es-Safi is a magnificent mound ; and were it unencumbered there would be no better site for the excavator in Palestine. But unfortunately the greater part of its contents are as inaccessible as though they were sealed with the inviolable seal of King Solomon. A large village of Arab fellahin, rendered crabbed in disposition by the malaria endemic in their unhealthy home, sprawls across the summit of the mound. The Crusaders here erected one of their castles—that known as Blanche-Garde; and although the fellahin have been diligent in pulling it down for its building stones, there was enough of it left to prevent digging, as a historical monument of the kind should not be totally destroyed. In any case, a Muslim saint had been buried close by, and had attracted to himself a modern cemetery of village worthies, whose graves must for a considerable time to come remain taboo. Similar cemeteries exist elsewhere on the mound, as well as the tombs of some other saints whose claims to sanctity, though they might possibly be disposed of by a well-briefed *advocatus diaboli*, are yet sufficiently strong to bar the door to science. When all these pre-empted areas are subtracted from the mound, the proportion left for the benefit of the excavator is very small indeed. It is therefore not surprising that the excavation of Tell es-Safi did not produce results commensurate with the size of the mound, and with the evident importance of the ancient city which it represents.

Still, the excavation was not wholly barren. A considerable length of the city wall was traced. A Canaanite sanctuary was unearthed, consisting of an enclosure with three (probably originally seven) unhewn pillar-stones standing in a row. A remarkable rubbish-heap was found in a re-entrant angle of the wall, containing an odd assortment of heterogeneous works of art—if, indeed, we may apply a term so respectful to objects so despicable. These consisted of fragments of terra-cotta figures, some of them indicating a coarse depravity of taste ; fragments of stone statuettes ; miscellaneous beads and amulets of Egyptian origin ; a curious plaque, with carving upon it in an Assyrian style ; some beads and seal-stones, in agate and similar ornamental stones ; half of a mould for casting small bronze bells and their clappers ; and a number of other odds and ends of pottery, etc. Evidently lost or waste objects had here been dumped ; the rubbish-heap of the city had stood at this spot. It is noteworthy, as an illustration of the continuity of tradition, that the modern village dumped its rubbish just above.

This fact has an important bearing on the site of the Church of the Holy Sepulchre. If it is authentic, it must have stood in just such a re-entrant angle of the walls of Jerusalem. The Crucifixion took place close by Joseph's garden, in which garden was the tomb which Joseph had intended for himself—and, in all probability, ultimately occupied. But a place where a rubbish-heap was likely to accumulate —and such a rubbish-heap would be not merely a pile of broken statuettes and pottery, but in plain English, and in the most literal sense of the term, a dung-heap—such a place would not be a probable site for the garden of a rich man.

Tell Zakariya had been occupied from late Pre-Israelite times to the time of the Maccabees, as the pottery showed. The occupation of Tell es-Safi seems to have begun rather earlier, and continued onwards to Maccabean times: an argument against its identification with Gath. The usual Roman khirbeh at the foot of the tell represented a yet later occupation. Afterwards the summit was re-colonised by the Crusaders; there was a layer of house-buildings to be attributed to these intruders, in addition to the remains of their castle of Blanche-Garde.

Tell el-Judeideh, the mound next attacked, has not certainly been identified with any ancient city. It proved to be a long narrow enclosure, with an acropolis at its southern end, having two gates. There were three strata of occupation, Pre-Israelite, Hebrew, and Maccabean; in addition a strongly-built house, probably of the Roman period, stood in the middle. The chief yield of the excavation at this place was a considerable number of jar-handles, sealed with the names of their makers in Old-Hebrew script; indeed, there were so many of these as almost to suggest that here was a centre of the pot-making industry. The large house in the middle was fully excavated, and its plan completely determined, but nothing whatever was found within it to give a clue to the personality of the owner.

Here, as at Tell Zakariya, the sides of the hill, and of others in the neighbourhood, were honeycombed with caves and rock-cuttings of various kinds. Deep cisterns, chambers with labyrinthine passages connecting them, and columbaria were in abundance, presenting problems more easily posed than answered. As a side-study in connexion with the excavation, a large number of these rock-cuttings were explored, measured, and mapped. But they deserve to be more than a mere side-study; they could profitably be made the subject for a special expedition, and extensive excavation should be carried out in the intensely hard dried mud that cumbers their floors. It cannot be claimed that in the more or less casual exploration, which they received during the expedition under discussion, any final solution of the problems which they present was reached.

The name of Tell Sandahannah, the fourth and last of the tells examined during this campaign of Dr. Bliss, is a corruption of *Sancta Anna*, to which saint a church built by the Crusaders in the neighbourhood was dedicated. The apse of this church still remained at the time of the exploration; but whether there is any vestige of it now surviving is a question which the present writer cannot answer. The large village of Beit Jibrin, the ancient Eleutheropolis, is close by, and its people would feel no delicacy in taking stones from this venerable ruin if they should happen to want to build a cow-shed. The tell represents the Greek city of Marissa, the earlier Moresheth, where the prophet Micah had his home. The name has been transferred, as is almost usual, in Roman times, to a new site, now represented by a khirbeh called Merash.

The excavation here was unfortunately cut short by the expiry of the permit. During the short time that Dr. Bliss was able to devote to this very attractive mound, the whole of the uppermost stratum was exposed and planned. Only one sounding was made into the lower strata, enough to show that the Hebrew Moresheth is there, awaiting the full excavation that it merits. In the upper city some very important finds were made, including a curious series of imprecatory and magical tablets, as well as part of an inscription of Arsinoe.

Here, once more, were many caves ; indeed, Tell Sandahannah may almost be called the centre of that strange city of artificial caves, which spreads over the hills around Beit Jibrin. The caves of Tell Sandahannah are hewn in the soft chalky limestone of which the hills are composed, and as at the other places which have been named, they consist of chambers united by doors and passages. For the greater part they are excavated with very little art ; but some chambers are not without an imposing grandeur. One cave was planned which contained no less than sixty chambers, large and small ; and caves with ten or even twenty chambers were found to be quite frequent. The most remarkable is a columbarium, consisting of a passage about 93 feet long, 4 feet 8 inches broad, and 22 feet high, with two transepts crossing it at intervals. The walls are divided into panels, containing groups of pigeon-holes, to the total number of 1906. These are rather too small for cinerary urns ; on the other hand, the cutting seems rather too elaborate to be a mere pigeon-house ; it is indeed a baffling place south, to which region research had hitherto been confined. There were the same rude huts crowded within strong walls, containing the same kinds of pottery and commonplace utensils. There was the same complete absence of any evidence of a native-born civilisation. There were the same hideous figures of the Semitic mother-goddess, that appear in large numbers in all the mounds. Some valuable finds for the study of Canaanite religion were found here, as will appear in the proper place, as well as a cache of cuneiform tablets of considerable importance. The first discovery in Palestine of jar-buried infants was made at Taanach. Probably the most remarkable of all Dr. Sellin's finds was a unique altar of earthenware, decorated with grotesque animal figures, which we shall describe later.

At about the same time the Palestine Exploration Fund began the excavation of Gezer. This site had been identified some thirty years before by Prof. Clermont-Ganneau, then officially resident in Jerusalem. He first discovered the mound, being led to search for it by a reference to it in the Arabic history of Mujir-ed-Din; and, shortly afterwards, he found a series of inscriptions cut in the outcrops of rock surrounding the hill, bearing in Hebrew the words "boundary of Gezer," and in Greek letters the name of a certain Alkios, presumably the governor of the city under whose auspices the inscriptions were cut. The excavation of this mound occupied five years (1902–5, 1906–8), in which time something over three-fifths of the total area had

THE SITE OF GEZER—IN THE BACKGROUND: IN THE FOREGROUND IS THE THRESHING-FLOOR OF THE MODERN VILLAGE.

been dug over. The remains covered all periods from the Neolithic age to the time of the Maccabees; a long series of objects and of structures, illustrative of cult and of culture was unearthed. A number of tombs were opened, but nothing was found comparable with the great Apollophanes tomb that had been so unfortunately missed at Sandahannah. Throughout the whole of the mound, from every stage of the city's history, much evidence of Egyptian influence came to light. As at other places, a khirbeh in the neighbourhood represented the Roman city; but here, contrary to the rule, the tell retains the ancient name, which was not transferred to the khirbeh site. The modern names are respectively *Tell el-Jezari* and *Khirbet Yerdeh.*

While the excavation of Gezer was in progress two new collaborators joined in the work: Germany and America. Germany, represented by Dr. Schumacher, an architect long resident in Palestine, who had already done most useful survey work, attacked Tell Mutasellim, a mound near to the site of Taanach, and representing that city's sister-town Megiddo. The excavation of this site was carried out on behalf of the Deutsche Palästina-Verein, with the co-operation of the Orient-Gesellschaft, and under the direct patronage of the German Emperor. Here, once more, the same comparatively low culture presented itself. No one, looking at the wretched huts which the excavation exposed, could possibly guess that from this very city Tahutmes III had carried off the great store of treasures which that acquisitive monarch enumerates in his records. This is a point of some importance, to which we shall have occasion to return. The find at Megiddo which created the greatest sensation was a seal of jasper, bearing a well-executed figure of a lion and a Hebrew inscription meaning "Belonging to Shema, servant of Jeroboam." It is generally supposed that the Jeroboam named was actually the second king of that name. Another seal, of lapis lazuli, was hardly less interesting; it bore a composite monstrous figure, an inscription in meaningless imitation Egyptian hieroglyphs, and another in Hebrew, indicating the seal as "Belonging to Asaph."

It is noteworthy that so far as excavation has hitherto shown, the "royal stamps" are confined to the south; none of them have been found in Northern Palestine.

At about the same time a minor excavation was carried out which, although not extensive, was of great importance for the history of the Jewish people. This was the clearance of the sites of the ancient synagogues of Galilee, and their systematic examination by Drs. Thiersch, Kohl, and Watzinger. The two last-named scholars had also been engaged in the clearance of the temple of Baalbec, a work which was one of the *sequelæ* of the German Emperor's pilgrimage to Palestine in 1898. Another consequence of that picturesque episode was less commendable; namely, the excision of a section of the rich façade of the palace of Mashitta, and its transference to Berlin. No doubt it is safer in Berlin than it was when exposed to the tender mercies of Bedawin and of occasional tourist souvenir-hunters. No doubt many hundreds can now see its gracious carving for one who could have seen it in its own setting. But the romance of that weird building, in its lonely grandeur amid the desert wastes, was so deeply impressive, that only the most pressing necessity (which does not appear to have been alleged) could possibly have justified the vandalism of disturbing it. But the Sultan presented it to the Kaiser, so there is no use in shedding tears over spilt milk.

To return to the synagogues, from which we have been diverted, these interesting structures seem to have first attracted attention during the progress of the Survey of Palestine. Lieut. Kitchener paid special attention to them, and determined the plan on which they were usually built. After the Baalbec work was finished Kohl and Watzinger visited most of them, and cleared their foundations, making it possible for the first time to study their remarkable ornament. The synagogue of Capernaum has been for some time in the especial charge of the Franciscan Order, and a sumptuous volume has recently been issued describing the results of their excavation of that important building.

America chose Samaria for its field of operations; work there was conducted first by Dr. D. G. Lyon, and afterwards by Dr. George Reisner, on behalf of Harvard University. This excavation was carried out on the large scale possible only to excavators well backed by a generous millionaire. It was rewarded by the discovery of most important buildings, notably the foundations of the palaces of Omri and of Ahab, as well as later structures of great interest. Most noteworthy was a great collection of ostraca; that is, potsherds, written upon with ink, in Old Hebrew characters. These were receipts and other documents relating to business transactions; they threw more than one ray of light on the social history of the time of the Israelite monarchy.

In 1908 Dr. Sellin, who had by now left Vienna and returned to Germany, once more visited Palestine, and in company with Drs. Langenegger and Watzinger, began a systematic examination of the remains of ancient Jericho. It cannot be said that this excavation, carefully though it was conducted, was very fruitful in results. By this time the general course of civilisation in the country had been fairly well determined. Excavators knew what were the ordinary daily utensils which would form their chief harvest. Types and forms were beginning to recur monotonously. As each new excavation is undertaken, more and more do *exceptional* things become desirable; for by now we can learn little from the perpetual recurrence of milk-bowls and cooking-pots. In this respect Jericho proved to be an essentially "ordinary" mound.

Much the same is true of Beth-Shemesh, now represented by Ain esh-Shems, the next scene of the operations of the Palestine Exploration Fund, directed by Dr. Duncan Mackenzie (1912-13). This site yielded some interesting tomb- and cave-groups of deposited objects, including many scarabs and beads, as well as some strangely rude statuettes. But there was here again little that was new or exceptional. A seal in a stone resembling porphyry was inscribed with two lines of Hebrew, but it has not been satisfactorily deciphered; it seems to say "Belonging to Chab (?) son of Badiel."

With the close of the excavation of Beth-Shemesh the record of excavation in Palestine, down to the beginning of the great war of 1914–18 comes to an end. It is outside our scope to speak of Mackenzie and Newton's survey of Petra, or of Woolley and Lawrence's exploration of the Wilderness of Zin. During the distractions of the world at war, scientific excavation anywhere would have been impossible; in any case it would have been completely impossible in Palestine, which was directly involved in the conflict. The war passed, and left a new Palestine, faced with new prospects and new ideals. The Turkish domination was gone; its place was taken by the British mandatory. Early in this new régime a properly equipped Department of Antiquities was established, charged with the duties of surveying, recording, and preserving the ancient remains of the country; of facilitating legitimate research; and of checking illegitimate digging for commercial purposes. The local authorities of the Turkish Government had established a Municipal Museum during the early years of the present century: perhaps less for the benefit of public instruction than because they were distressed that a possible source of personal emolument should depart out of their reach to Constantinople. A considerable number of the objects from the excavations in the Philistine Plain, and from Gezer, had been deposited in this museum. The new Department took over, arranged, and classified what was left of this museum; its contents had not *all* been stolen in the meanwhile. At the same time a British School of Archæology was founded in Jerusalem, thus bringing Great Britain into line with France, America, and Germany. These countries had founded flourishing schools of Archæology, Semitics, and Theology even under the Turkish régime, giving students the opportunity of acquiring a first-hand acquaintance with the country, its antiquities and its languages.

So soon as Palestine was once more open to science, a new impetus was given to research. No longer would the excavator have to face the heart-breaking delays of a procrastinating government, and the seemingly arbitrary difficulties put in his way by both the central and the local authorities of the Turk. We have seen already how the Palestine Exploration Fund was refused permission to excavate an unimportant site that happened to have a similar name to the town of Ascalon. The alleged reason was that at Ascalon there were Holy Places, which the projected work would disturb. Probably the real reason was that as Ascalon is near the sea, it was supposed that smuggling of antiquities out of the country would be too easy; perhaps there was also a suspicion that, under cover of excavating, the explorer might throw up trenches and mounds that would hereafter be useful for military operations. In a country where electric light was forbidden, because it required a *dynamo*, which was too suspiciously like *dynamite* to be admissible, an explorer learnt early to be prepared for many such unexpected misrepresentations of his motives. It is an amusing commentary on this amusing episode that the first place to be excavated, after the war was over, was Ascalon itself. It had been examined and reported upon before the war by Dr. Mackenzie ; and the work was begun as soon as possible by the Palestine Exploration Fund and the British School jointly, under the control of Dr. Garstang, the director of the British School and head of the Department of Antiquities.

The site is especially attractive. The field of remains is extensive, the accumulation deep, the surface unencumbered. The city has played an important part in history, from the days of the Philistines to those of the Crusaders. Its connexion with the Philistines gave reason to hope that its excavation would throw some fresh light on those mysterious people.

But unfortunately these expectations were disappointed. The time was not propitious for so extensive a work. Money, in colloquial phrase, was tight ; there was little to spare for science. Without more thousands of pounds than were available in the lean years that followed the war, the Philistine stratum could not be reached, on account of its depth : moreover, it was overlaid with a series of Herodian buildings of historical importance, the removal of which could be justified only by the most urgent necessity.

Not more than a passing mention is needed of the excavation of Tell el-Ful, north of Jerusalem, by Dr. Albright of the American School of Archæology. This site had long been identified with Gibeah of Saul. The excavation does not appear to have been very productive; nothing bearing on this identification, for or against, was discovered.

The Jewish aspirations with regard to Palestine naturally look backward as well as forward. It is not to be expected that they would allow "Gentiles" to garner all the field of historical research. An EXPLORATION SOCIETY has been founded since the war among the Jewish colonists in Palestine, and a Jewish Museum opened. This society publishes a journal in the Hebrew language. Under the superintendence of Dr. Nahum Slousch it conducted an examination of the ancient synagogue of Tiberias. As we write Dr. Slousch has been clearing the accumulation of stones and earth away from the base of the well-known Herodian tomb called "Absalom's Pillar" in the Kidron Valley. By this useful work the full proportions of this strange monument can be seen for the first time. It is a great pity that a natural flaw in the rock of which the plinth is made spoils the æsthetic effect of the façade of the tomb; but otherwise it looks much more imposing than it did when partly buried under some six or eight feet of rubbish. At the back of the tomb Dr. Slousch has exposed to light the once well-known Herodian tomb called by the ridiculous name, "Tomb of Jehoshaphat." It is a cause for deep regret that the large numbers of modern Jewish graves, thickly scattered around this and the companion monuments in the Kidron Valley, hamper Dr. Slousch's work, and especially that they prevent him from laying bare the whole of the adjacent "Pyramid of Zacharias." There can hardly fail to be a tomb-chamber inside this monument, but the entrance thereto has never been seen in modern times. It is also unfortunate that some highly imaginative descriptions of discoveries made by Dr. Slousch have gone the round of the Press, and have obscured the real nature, and the real value, of his work.

At the point where the angle of the Plain of Esdraelon impinges upon the Jordan valley, there is one of the prize sites of Palestine: Beisan, the Biblical Beth-Shean. The site is a wide-spread field of ruins, surrounding a superb mound that bears the name Tell el-Husn. This mound represents the walled area of the Canaanite city, and the acropolis of the Scythian and Hellenistic city of Scythopolis, the successor of Beth-Shean on this site. Excavation began here in 1922, under the direction of Mr. Clarence S. Fisher, on behalf of the University Museum of Philadelphia. In his first reports, which are all that have come to hand at the moment of writing, he describes having sunk a trial shaft in this mound, to a depth of 36 feet, without reaching rock. In this shaft he passed through a number of strata, ranging in date from 2000 B.C.

to A.D. 800. In a subsequent clearance on the site he uncovered no less than eight strata in the first 20–30 feet, reaching at that depth a brick fortress of the time of Seti I (1313–1292 B.C.). Its wall in some places stood to a height of 10 feet. Inside this fortress were found commemorative stelæ of Seti I and Ramessu II, with long hieroglyphic inscriptions, as well as a seated statue of Ramessu III. All of these monuments were locally made, of the basalt of the district. Another Seti I stele was found in a later stratum; it had been stolen from the fortress, to make a door-sill. Besides these inscriptions, unique in Palestine, the foundation of a very early church, of the Basilica plan, claiming to be the oldest church site yet found in the east, was uncovered; it had a mosaic floor. This work at Beisan has practically only just begun, and is being carried out on the sumptuous scale which seems to be possible only to American excavating parties. In such a site anything may come to light; there is no limit to its possibilities.

Finally we have to speak of three more excavations which, as we write, are still in progress at Jerusalem. The first is an extensive work which has been carried out for a considerable time by the Assumptionist Fathers, on land belonging to them on the Western Hill; this will, it is hoped, reveal important facts regarding the Jerusalem of the Gospels. The second is the excavation conducted for the Baron de Rothschild at the south end of the Eastern Ridge by Capt. Raymond Weill. This work was begun

THE SITE OF BETH-SHEAN.

before the war, and has since been resumed. The upper end of the ridge had not been touched since Warren's time, except in a few soundings made by Guthe, which were too disconnected to give any coherent information, and in some tunnelling by the Hon. Capt. Parker, who accomplished the useful service of cleaning out the Siloam Tunnel. But in 1924 the third excavation, involving a clearance in this part of the site, began under a former director of the work of the Palestine Exploration Fund, assisted by the Rev. J. G. Duncan, a minister of the Church of Scotland. The topographical and other results of these investigations are set forth in the following chapters.

CHAPTER II

EXCAVATION AND TOPOGRAPHY

A THOROUGH grasp of the geographical setting of any historical narrative is almost always necessary for its full comprehension. We cannot form a true mental picture of a scene, recorded as taking place within the four walls of a building, unless we have some knowledge of the architectural character of the building, its size, and the disposition of its furniture. We cannot follow the details of a battle without being informed as to the configuration of the ground upon which it has taken place. We cannot trace the advance of an exploring expedition without a map of its line of route.

This principle applies to Biblical as well as to secular history. The stories in the Old Testament are miracles of condensation. Surely there is no literature in the world that tells so much in so few words. But this necessarily involves the omission of descriptive matter, which the readers originally contemplated could have supplied for themselves, but which for us, at our distance of time and of space, cannot be called common knowledge. A modern writer, wishing to introduce into his narrative such an incident as the death of Samson, would have interpolated a chapter, explaining, probably with diagrams, the construction of the temple in which the catastrophe took place. The Book of Judges tells us the essential parts of the story, and leaves it to its readers to find out, as best they can, where the crowds watching the feats of the strong man were seated, and how it came about that the displacement of two pillars brought down the entire structure.

A narrative will often turn essentially upon a point of topography. Every now and then we are confronted with a question—which naturally varies with the narrative, but which may be of some such type as these: Is this the kind of place where an army could be ambushed? Is such-and-such a place visible from this mountain-top? It follows that the identification of sites is a matter of the first importance for the explanation of the Biblical record. This is true of the identification of cities and villages; of valleys, springs, and mountains; and of specific sites within the area of any given city.

The determination of the sites of cities and of villages may be called the problem of *major topography*; the establishment of identifications of buildings, and of the scenes of events within a single city, may be called *minor topography*. On the whole, the former is of less account than the latter in a study of the bearings of excavation upon topography; for as a rule excavation has been undertaken only in sites which had already been identified, with greater or less certainty, before their examination began. The only important exception was Tell el-Judeideh; and even this was examined on the chance that it might prove to be the missing Gath.

There are two reasons for this. In the first place, if something is already known of the history of a site, there is a better chance of identifying the footprints of history in its dust-heaps, and of adding thereby to our knowledge of chronology. In the second place, there is the practical consideration that excavation is a very expensive pursuit, and depends on the support and goodwill of subscribers. It must be confessed that, to the majority of subscribers, pure science, as such, makes but little appeal. If it were advertised that investigation was contemplated in some Palestinian mound which it was as yet impossible to identify with a Biblical site, the public would take the announcement rather coldly. Closed would be the purse-strings, that would open to an appeal to examine some place connected with Abraham or with David, even though this might hold out less promise of important results than the other. It is melancholy to have to add that any legitimate undertaking would be less widely and generously supported than something crudely spectacular, such as an expedition to find the Lost Ten Tribes, or the Ark of the Covenant, or Joseph's Coat of Many Colours.

Down to about a hundred years ago, only the chief sites were certainly known. By turning over the quaint maps in Fuller's *Pisgah-sight of Palestine* we can see that for students of his time the great survey of the country, summarised in the middle of the Book of Joshua, had no real relation to the actual profile of the land. Robinson's work of re-discovery was continued by the officers of the Ordnance Survey. In the year 1895 the Palestine Exploration Fund published a list of *Names and Places in the Old and New Testaments and the Apocrypha, with their Modern Identifications*, compiled by the Assistant Secretary of the Fund at the time, Mr. George Armstrong, from the materials collected by the Survey. According to the preface to this work, it contains upwards of 1,150 names in the section relating to the Old Testament and the Apocrypha, 162 names in the New Testament section. Most of these belong to places in Palestine, though there are others in Egypt, Asia Minor, and Mesopotamia, and a few in Europe. We are further told that 290 of the Old Testament names, and 8 of the New Testament names, are " Not Identified." But the number of unidentified sites is really more considerable. Many of the identifications that have been proposed, and that are accepted in the compilation here analysed, cannot be sustained. The work of identification needs to be revised from the beginning, and tested by critical touchstones that were not available when the Survey was made.

Let us consider the arguments on which the identification of a Biblical site in Palestine must rest. In the first place, it must fit all the topographical conditions that are deducible from the

the ground. And truly the fantastic idea might almost be called justifiable. All round Jerusalem we may pick up fragments of Roman pottery by the score, with but little expenditure of time and trouble. Now, Roman pottery necessarily implies the presence of Romans, or, at least, of people under the influence of Roman culture. If there are no earlier sherds to be found on a site, then there was no occupation of earlier date, and if we are searching for a Pre-Roman site, we must look elsewhere.

More direct evidence of identification is rare in Palestine. The best of all forms of evidence is the discovery, on the site, of an inscription containing the name of the city. In Palestine this has happened only twice: at Gezer, in the boundary stones, and at Marissa, in the tomb of Apollophanes. Less direct evidence is afforded by the Lachish tablet, with its mention of Zimrida, known from other sources to have been governor of Lachish. Old milestones are sometimes useful, if they are found in their true position; they must be the specified distance from the sites that happen to be named upon them.

At the present moment much valuable work is being done by the British and American Archæological Schools in Palestine in testing the old identifications by archæological evidence. When this work is complete many of the details of our Biblical maps will have to be revised. To name but a few of the still outstanding problems of major topography, we still need certainty as to the sites of Gath and Ekron, among important places mentioned in the Old Testament; of many of the places mentioned in the lists of Tahutmes III and in the Tell el-Amarna letters; of sundry places referred to in the narrative of the Maccabean wars, such as Dathema, Alema, Casphor, and Maked; and, among notable New Testament sites, of Emmaus. Five or six villages have been identified with this place; the only thing certain is that the village of *Amwas*, which bears something like the old name, is much too far away from Jerusalem to be the true site.

Contrariwise, there are a few striking sites, showing relics of ancient occupation, which it has not yet been found possible to equate to any recorded town or village of antiquity.

But it is in the region of what we have just called *minor topography* that excavation has chiefly touched upon topographical problems. Naturally, most of this work has been carried out in and near Jerusalem.

Jerusalem is a small place; but years could be spent in studying even its surface topography. To investigate its rubbish-heaps thoroughly would cost well over a million sterling, and would give a life's work to several generations of archæologists.

If a visitor to Jerusalem wishes to gain an intelligent insight into the relation between the history of the city and its remains, even though he may not care to enter deeply into the *minutiæ* of the subject, he must be prepared for at least a month's hard work inside the city, supplemented by a long course of reading in special treatises. The great majority of those who come out in his mind the labyrinthine plan of the Church itself. Each new site will drive out everything more than a confused recollection of its predecessor. His guide will in the meanwhile labour to impart information about the Empress Helena, not always with unqualified success ; I have known of tourists confusing that lady with the Queen Eleanor of whom they have a vague recollection from history-lessons at school. With the architectural history of the Church itself neither tourist nor guide will make any effort to grapple ; perhaps fortunately. The traveller will leave the Church a-maze ; before he has had time to recover himself he will be conducted to a nunnery hard by, and will there be shown some venerable fragments of ruined walls. It would be quite impossible for anyone who has not made a special study of the Church of the Holy Sepulchre, and of its complex history, to form the least idea of what these walls are ; certainly the *dux cæcus cæci* at our tourist's elbow is not qualified to explain them. Leaving this house of mystery, he is hurried, so far as the jostling crowds make hurry possible, through another street, full of minor points of interest (but it is unlikely that he will see any of these) to what he is told is the Damascus Gate. The Damascus Gate is a concentration of all the problems of Jerusalem topography. Everything turns primarily upon its relation to the original north wall, and upon the identification of the ancient gateway that can be traced, incorporated in its Saracenic masonry. As an architectural monument it is well worthy of careful study for its own sake. But time presses ; the tourist is, we had almost written, frog-marched through this venerable portal ; a hillock to the right is pointed out—with a carelessness of manner that must surely be shocking to any thoughtful traveller's sense of reverence—as " Gordon's Calvary " ; and the morning's sight-seeing ends at what he is told is " Gordon's Tomb."

Such is a picture of half a day in the life of a modern tourist in Jerusalem. Except for one important difference, it might serve as a picture of a few hours in the life of any mediæval pilgrim, from the days when an unknown wanderer from Bordeaux, the first to write an account of his experiences, came to worship in the year of the Lord 333. This difference is the total elimination of the devotional element ; and the difference is fundamental. The pilgrim came for the sake of his religion ; the tourist comes for mere curiosity. To the pilgrim, a visit to the Holy Land in general, and to the Holy City in particular, was the central experience of his whole life ; to the tourist it is a mere incident in a round trip, which he has taken in luxurious ease, and most of which he has forgotten six months later. The pilgrim was guided by an ecclesiastic who had renounced the world (at least in theory) ; the tourist is guided by a dragoman who renounces nothing that he can lay his hands on. The pilgrim carried away a glowing sense of sins forgiven and a soul saved ; the tourist carries away a bag full of serviette-rings, and candlesticks, and models of camels, and the like rubbish in polished olive-wood, which lumber the course of the present city wall to that of the wall at the beginning of the Christian era.

But while such scepticism is pardonable—we might almost say justifiable—it is quite a different matter to suggest a rival site. Scepticism is nothing less than a duty, if it be arrived at fairly by a process of logical reasoning, and is not a mere expression of prejudice against what is abusively called "monkishness" and "mummery." When the sceptic proceeds to display a credulity no less unreasonable, in favour of some arbitrarily selected site of his own, he forfeits all claim to serious attention. It cannot be said too strongly, or too often, that our only literary sources of information do not give us sufficient data for determining *de novo* the site of the Crucifixion and of the Entombment of Christ. If we reject tradition, then we know not whether those events happened north, south, east, or west of the city; though we may legitimately say that the east is the least probable direction owing to the contour of the ground. If we reject the site that was determined by, or for, the Empress Helena, and that has been hallowed by the reverence of millions during the centuries that have intervened, we must be content to remain in complete ignorance. Destructive criticism of tradition is sometimes necessary; to establish a new, mushroom tradition is to commit an outrage on both religion and science. Nothing short of the very improbable discovery of a demonstrably authentic and contemporary inscription could be accepted as satisfactory evidence of any other tomb.

There are many, many things that a true lover of Jerusalem would gladly see abolished ; the cult of this absurd pseudo-sanctuary called " Gordon's Tomb," or " The Garden Tomb," is the first of them. Its site, however, has genuine claims to be preserved as a historical monument. Here there once stood an erection of great importance, and of much greater usefulness than many a more pretentious structure. It was the building in which the Crusaders stabled their asses.

We have dwelt on this matter longer perhaps than it merits, because it is one of the best available illustrations of the wrong way of attacking topographical problems. The treatment of such questions should be as rigid and as free from all emotion as the discussion of a question in mathematics. In the present case, the position is something like this. Good people are repelled, very naturally, by the scandalous disputes of imperfect humanity in the Church of the Holy Sepulchre. They also observe that its authenticity would involve a singular readjustment of the course of the city walls—though it is sometimes hard to make out how far discussion of the walls is affected subjectively by prepossessions as to the authenticity or otherwise of the Church site. Being persuaded that the Church site must be wrong, they seek another. A new Calvary and a new Holy Sepulchre must be found. The former is ready to their hands, in a hillock outside the Damascus Gate ; and as two caves side by side on its face give it a curious resemblance to a skull, they find at once an obvious interpretation for the name *Golgotha*. It is without the wall of the modern city ; and it fits the conception of the appearance of Calvary which has been instilled into the English mind from childhood by the familiar hymn beginning :

> There is a green hill far away,
> Without a city wall . . .

But others arrive at the same result by a different route. That strange mystic General Gordon was not impressed with the external resemblance which this hill bears to a skull. He had an idea that the emplacement of Jerusalem was a kind of typical picture of a human body ; a drawing made by him is extant, showing a skeleton laid out with its head at the " Skull Hill," its waist at the Holy Rock in the Haram area, and its feet at the Pool of Siloam. This is the reason for the association of the name of Gordon with this hill. Of the tomb, to which his name is transferred, there is no evidence that he took any notice whatever.

It is not by nebulous speculations of this kind that prosaic topographical problems can be solved in this matter-of-fact world. All such fantastic dreams carry with them their own condemnation. But even the less imaginative arguments for the hill outside the Damascus Gate make a mere house of cards, which it is not difficult to demolish. Absolutely *fatal* to its claim is the mere fact that it is a hill. This may come as a surprise ; have we not always thought of *Mount* Calvary ? Yet there is not the slightest warrant for this in any of the Gospel narratives. On the contrary, we have the direct testimony of Quintilian to the Roman practice of erecting the cross, in cases of execution by crucifixion, *on a way-side*, in order to act as a deterrent from crime by making the fullest possible exposition of the horrors of this mode of punishment—just as in England highwaymen were formerly hanged on gibbets erected on public highways, for the same purpose. That the crucifixion of Christ was no exception to this rule is quite clear. In the account in Mark xv. 29, we read how casual passers-by added their contribution of insult to the Sufferer, as they went on their way. There is not, and could not be, any road over the " Skull Hill " ; passers-by on the adjacent roads would have had to take the trouble of shouting at the tops of their voices in order to make themselves heard.

The hill has been reduced to its present shape artificially, by quarrying. The two eye-sockets, so called, are in the face of a vertical scarp. They are cisterns, which have been broken out by the quarrying operations. The hill was of a different shape, and the buildings to which these cisterns belonged were still standing, when Sandys visited Palestine early in the seventeenth century ; they are shown in a bird's-eye view of Jerusalem on p. 158 of his *Relation of a Journey*, here reproduced from my own copy of the third edition, published in 1627. Thus the skull-like aspect of the hill is comparatively modern, and cannot be used to connect with it an ancient name of unknown significance.

Such, then, is a good example of false method in topographical identification. We must now turn to a more scientific treatment of problems of this nature.

The fact of primary importance, which must ever be borne in mind in studying Jerusalem topography, is the complete break made as a result of the siege of Titus. The city was utterly destroyed, save for a few buildings, such as Herod's Palace, preserved in part for administrative purposes. The new Jerusalem which rose from the ashes of the city that Herod and Pilate and Caiaphas had known, was an altogether new creation. The highways leading to the city were unchanged, so that the city gates approximately maintained their old positions. This ensured that some of the streets inside the walls should follow the old lines ; but otherwise a survivor from the old city would find nothing familiar in the new.

Next, we must remember that even Titus's destruction was not the last. Roman, Byzantine, Arab, Crusader, and Turk have in turn made themselves masters of the city, and in so doing they have added to the rubbish-heaps cumbering the site. Old walls are ruthlessly pulled down for the sake of the building-stones, whenever the buildings to which they belonged have served their purpose ; so that even the reconstruction after Titus is itself buried under a heap of later accumulation. Without excavation the recovery of the ancient city is perfectly impossible ; and

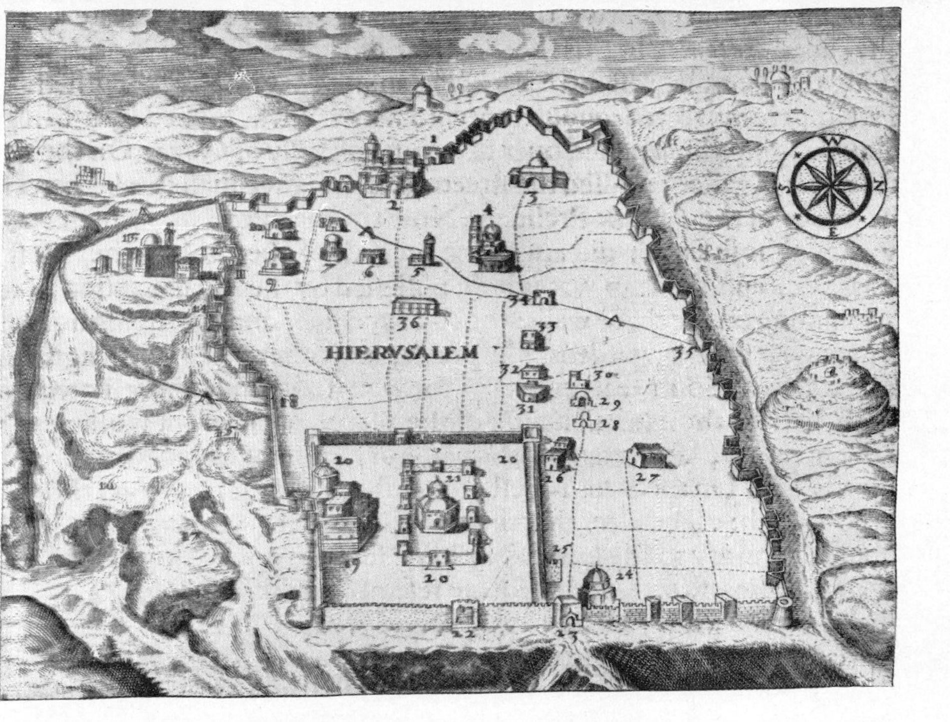

BIRD'S EYE VIEW OF JERUSALEM, SHOWING THE APPEARANCE OF THE SO-CALLED "SKULL HILL" IN THE SEVENTEENTH CENTURY (THE CONSPICUOUS CONICAL HILL UNDERNEATH THE COMPASS).

excavation in a crowded city, with property-owners disinclined to further the excavator's work, is very far from easy.

Let us consider the chief problems in chronological order. They may be stated thus :

(1) The position of the Jebusite city, afterwards called "The City of David."

(2) The nature of the fortifications and extensions under David, Solomon, and succeeding kings.

(3) The course of Nehemiah's wall.

(4) The sacred sites of the Gospels.

There are in addition not a few questions relating to the Jerusalem of the Arabs and the Crusaders, but these must here be passed by. It is needless to say that in the space available for us only the most superficial account can be given of researches about which large volumes have been, and will yet be, written.

The Position of the Jebusite City

For those who would seek for the Jerusalem of Melchi-zedek and of Abd-Khiba, of Adoni-Zedek and of David, the fact of capital importance is the presence of the so-called Virgin's Fountain, the only natural source of water in the neighbourhood of Jerusalem. This is an intermittent spring, rising in a cave in the Kidron Valley, a little to the south of the present emplacement of the city. There was also a cave, or rather a rift, in the hilltop above, which at a very remote date yielded water ; but it early became choked. This left the Virgin's Fountain as the solitary place where water was to be had, until cisterns were dug, and until the great shaft of Job's Well, a little further down the valley, had been constructed, to collect the filtration of the waters of the three valleys.

It follows that the early shepherd-nomads, whom we may presume to have been the first dwellers on the site of Jerusalem, must have established their tents or their huts as near to the cave of the Virgin's Fountain as possible. It is exceedingly difficult to make a mental picture of the aspect of the site before human occupation began, so completely has the profile of the landscape been changed by the accumulation of miscellaneous debris. The Kidron is the most easterly of the three deep, steep valleys—abrupt trenches would almost be a better expression by which to describe them—which define or cut through the plateau on which the city stands, and which unite together at about the place where Job's Well is now sunk. The most westerly of these valleys is identified with the valley of Hinnom; the central valley is that which Josephus has taught us to call the Tyropoeon Valley, that is, the Valley of Cheesemongers. This last-named valley is now all but completely filled with rubbish; and probably there is not much less than forty feet of rubbish covering the bed of the Kidron. If we wish to imagine it as it must have been when it was first inhabited, we must picture its sides as steeper—precipitous rocks, in fact; and the cave of the Virgin's Fountain, instead of being sunk as it is now, below the level of the ground,

THE KIDRON VALLEY, LOOKING NORTHWARD—MODERN JERUSALEM IN THE BACKGROUND ON THE LEFT, THE SITE OF THE JEBUSITE CITY IN FRONT OF IT. THE VILLAGE OF SILWAN ON THE RIGHT.

must have been at some height above the floor of the valley, and discharged its waters as a waterfall into the river-bed below. The rise of the water being intermittent, not continuous, and moreover taking place at irregular intervals, it was necessary to be on the watch for the outflow; and there was always the chance of losing the opportunity of obtaining a sufficiency owing to the quarrels for precedence which would be inevitable. To get rid of these inconveniences, the bottom of the cave was at an early date artificially deepened to make a reservoir, the water being reached by steps cut in the rock. After the accumulation of rubbish had buried the cave, this stair was continued upwards to the new surface of the earth by adding a number of steps in masonry. The Arabic name of the spring is therefore one which means "The Staircase Spring."

Warren's excavations showed that there was another watercourse in the bed of the Tyropoeon Valley; but most likely it was fed by the winter rains, and was not a perennial stream. In this connexion it is, however, necessary to interpolate a word of caution. We cannot assume that the climate of modern Palestine can be taken as identical with the climate of ancient Palestine. The researches of Prof. Elsworth Huntingdon have gone far to establish the existence of secular changes in this respect, of alternations of periods of heavy rainfall with periods of light rainfall; and therefore we should not speak, without reserve, of "winter torrents" and similar phenomena, such as are familiar in the Palestine of to-day. So far as we know, there was no spring to feed the Tyropoeon water-course during the time of human occupation. The elaborate system of conduits which have been found, derived from the Virgin's Fountain, shows us its paramount importance to the inhabitants of the city, and suggests that it was their only spring.

It is therefore natural to look for the earliest city of Jerusalem as near to the Virgin's Fountain as possible; that is to say, on the spur between the Kidron and the Tyropoeon Valleys. This runs counter to tradition, which has fixed the "City of Zion" on the Western Hill, between the Tyropoeon and the Hinnom Valleys. But although the Western Hill, on a superficial view, is far more suitable for the emplacement of a city, being broader and more commanding than the Eastern Hill, its lack of water is a fatal objection to its claims.

But clearly the rival claims of the two possible sites offer an admirable subject for the decision of the spade; and this was the chief problem attacked by the latest excavation at Jerusalem, under the joint auspices of the Palestine Exploration Fund and the *Daily Telegraph*, which began on the Eastern Hill in October, 1923.

This excavation revealed a small valley, tributary to the Tyropoeon, and cutting into the western side of the Eastern Hill, about 330 yards south of the nearest part of the modern city wall. Its position is close to a footpath which here runs across the hill, leading down to the bottom of the Kidron Valley from the modern

"Dung Gate." This valley had been excavated by a streamlet that had flowed from a cave on the summit of the hill in Tertiary times; but when human occupation began, this stream was already dry, and a very early interment was found to have been made inside the cave, even in the bed of the stream. This tributary valley had early been adapted as a fortification; its upper end, which was naturally of small dimensions, being enlarged, by quarrying, into a trench some ten feet wide and eight feet deep.

A city placed on the summit of the Eastern Hill would be well protected by the steep precipices of the surrounding valleys, except to the north. Here there was nothing to block the entrance of a hostile invader. It was for this reason that the artificial valley was cut through the crest of the hill. Although the puny efforts of man are insignificant beside the mighty works of nature, such a trench would be very effective in preventing the city from being captured by a rush.

This newly-discovered valley is therefore important topographically. It formed the northern boundary of the city, at a time when the eastern hill was first inhabited. It was found to be filled with debris, containing many potsherds dating about 1600 B.C. This gives a date for its supersession as a defence. It had then gone out of use, and was allowed to become filled up. We must probably allow several centuries, in the slow-moving East, for the term of usefulness of a work so important; its formation can hardly be later than about

water must always have had the inconvenience of going outside the city, and climbing down a steep path, to scramble up again laden with their heavy pitchers. In time of siege the spring would be not only inaccessible, but would be at the service of the enemy. Hezekiah's sensible question, " Why should the king of Assyria come and find much water ? " was doubtless asked, *mutatis mutandis*, by many of his predecessors in authority.

The inhabitants of the Jebusite city solved the problem by a grandiose scheme of rock-cutting, which they carried out effectively. A horizontal tunnel was driven back from the inner end of the cave to a certain distance. A vertical shaft was cut, breaking into the end of this tunnel. The shaft ended upward in the floor of a second horizontal passage above, which opened inside the area of the city. The upper passage is crooked, indicating that the excavators had some difficulty in determining the end of the position of the lower tunnel ; indeed, they opened a trial shaft just inside the entrance to the upper tunnel, which they sunk to a considerable depth before they discovered that it was much too far to the west. (It is also possible that this shaft was made afterwards, in order to stop the tunnel, after Joab's exploit had shown that it was a source of military weakness to the city. If it existed while the tunnel was in use as a water-passage, it must have been filled up with earth, as otherwise it would have been a very serious danger to those who made legitimate use of it.)

Similar installations have been found elsewhere in the country. The great tunnel of Gezer, one of the most important of the discoveries there made, was essentially of this character. A similar water-passage exists at Belameh, the site of Ibleam; and another at El-Jib, the ancient Gibeon. As excavation progresses doubtless others will be found.

We may reasonably ask the question why the Jebusites were content to settle on this single spur? They might have carried their city upward to the summit of the plateau, still protected by what was then the deep rift of the Tyropoeon Valley. Instead of their northern wall being some 200 yards south of the present city wall, it might have included the commanding height now crowned by the Haram esh-Sherif, where Solomon's Temple once stood.

It can hardly be questioned that they did not include the hill-top within their city because it was already holy ground. There is no reason to suppose that Solomon was the first to establish a sanctuary here. Very likely it had been consecrated to many strange gods, before it had become holy to the God of the Hebrews. It was therefore left respectfully alone, and did not become incorporated within the city until long afterwards. Moreover, we must always bear in mind the small size of ancient Palestinian cities. The first Jerusalem was the city of a small community; the triangle intercepted within the Kidron, the Tyropoeon, and the Zedek Valleys was amply sufficient room for its needs.

THE EXTENSIONS UNDER THE HEBREW KINGS

David took Jerusalem and made it his metropolis ; but he does not seem to have enlarged or beautified it in any way. He had no leisure for any such undertakings, although he had cherished dreams of building a permanent house for the reception of the Ark. His time was taken up with wars, and with the overwhelming troubles in his own family ; he was obliged to bequeath to his son and successor Solomon the task which was denied to himself.

When Solomon came to the throne he made a levy for the fortification of certain of his cities, including Jerusalem. There, we read, he repaired the breaches of David his father—the breaches in the wall which David had made in capturing the city, and which had been only temporarily patched up during David's long reign ; and built " Millo." Millo is occasionally mentioned in the subsequent record. The reader is assumed to know what this structure was, and is never told anything about it. Joash was murdered in the house of Millo ; a repair of Millo was one of the tasks undertaken by Hezekiah when he fortified the city, in preparation for the Assyrian menace. The house of Millo at Shechem, of which we read in the story of Abimelech (Judges ix), was clearly something quite different.

In the excavation of 1923–24 the following *ensemble* of remains of building was unearthed, a little to the north of the Zedek Valley :

(1) A rock-scarp running east and west,

SITE OF FORTRESS RECENTLY DISCOVERED AND IDENTIFIED WITH MILLO.

evidently forming part of an ancient line of defence.

(2) The remains of a wall which had run over this rock-scarp, and which had been violently breached.

(3) A long wall built inside the area included by this breached wall, masking the breach.

(4) A fortress tower built above the breach, filling the gap which it made in the wall, and using the fallen stones of the breach as a foundation.

(5) Some much later buildings, that had evidently been constructed out of materials taken from the foregoing structures, to their very serious detriment; in fact, very little of them was left.

Without going so far as to say that the identification of the fortress, number (4) in the above list, with Millo is mathematically demonstrable, and that it is quite impossible that there should still remain hidden, under the earth, some other site with a better claim to represent the work of Solomon, we may note that there are certain striking coincidences between the Biblical account and the remains observed. We need a breach in the wall, and we have it—a breach in the north wall of the Jebusite city, just where it would most likely be. Then we need this breach to remain for a considerable time, and this is obviously what has happened. Doubtless David laid an embargo on the fallen building-stones, intending to use them himself; otherwise they would have been cleared away within a few months. But David could not have left his city wall in its dilapidated condition, for any enemy to enter at will; he therefore drew a straight wall across the breached portion, as a temporary barricade. We read in II Samuel v that after taking the city he "built from Millo round about," which does not in the least imply that Millo, as such, was already in existence; it is as though the author said, "he built from where we, historian and reader, know Millo to stand at the present day." Thus interpreted, the passage might very well refer to the building of this barricade wall, which is, in fact, round about the site of the fortress which we identify with Millo. This wall was in a very peculiar masonry. It consisted of alternate courses of large and small stones. It was, in fact, just such a wall as might be run up hurriedly with the materials which the breached city wall supplied: very large stones, requiring the efforts of three or four strong men to move, trimmed down to a manageable size, and thus leaving the builders with large heaps of small splinters of broken stone to dispose of.

The radical meaning of the word "Millo" is "filling"; and it is appropriate to this fortress, which fills up the gap in the wall. We shall never know its complete plan, as Herodians and Byzantines were busy demolishing it to supply stones for their own constructions. But as though to strengthen yet further the connection between king Solomon and this structure, faint traces of a very rude painting of Ashtaroth were observed on one of the building stones, reminding us of the king's lapses into paganism.

Judgement must be suspended until every other likely or unlikely site has been examined; but for the meanwhile the recently discovered remains make a good claim to offer a solution of this much discussed topographical problem.

That the Temple of Solomon was erected somewhere within the area of the Haram esh-Sherif, miscalled the Mosque of Omar, is unquestioned and unquestionable. The actual position of the building within the area may be a little more open to dispute, but by far the most probable site is that occupied by the Dome of the Rock, built over the sacred rock of which so many stories are told—although in actual fact it is nothing more romantic than the apex of the underlying hill. Solomon's palace, south of the Temple, is probably represented in position by Justinian's great church of St. Mary, now, in a truncated form, the Mosque "el-Aksa." So long as these sanctuaries remain under the guardianship of a suspicious people, hostile to research, so long will it be impossible to seek for any relics of the Solomonic buildings. But even were it possible to make such a search, it is improbable that anything of the kind would be discovered. Nebuchadnezzar was nothing if not thorough; and Herod, when laying the foundation of his own ambitious structure, would have but scant courtesy for the work of his predecessor. The huge stones in the surrounding wall are doubtless Herodian in their present position, although they might well have been taken from the ruins of the Solomonic buildings. But it is as well to insist on the

In the year 1874 certain reconstructions had to be made in this building and its grounds ; in carrying out the work the architect, Henry Maudslay, laid bare a great rock-scarp, which had evidently formed part of an important fortification. Projecting from the main scarp is what has every appearance of having been the rock-cut base of a tower, standing on a lower stage of rock, which itself has a scarped face. On this rock-cut tower, which is some 45 feet square and 20 feet high, the school buildings are partly erected. From the tower the scarp runs northward, towards the south-west angle of the present city wall, in which direction it has been traced for 100 feet. In the opposite direction it runs southward from the tower for about 50 feet, after which it follows a south-easterly direction for about 350 feet, where another projecting tower is encountered. A flight of rock-cut steps in the face of the scarp near this second tower leads from the bottom of the scarp to the top. About midway between these two towers there is a smaller tower. Excavation outside this system revealed the fact that there was a rock-cut parapet, or curtain, drawn in front of the main scarp ; between the parapet and the main scarp there is a passage, fosse, or moat. We have therefore three walls of rock at this corner ; the outer scarp of the parapet, facing south-west; the inner scarp of the parapet, facing north-east ; and the main scarp which carried the fortification, again facing south-west.

The second of the two large towers, which was about the same size as the first, still retained some of its masonry when Bliss opened down on it. Outside this tower the rock-cut fosse continued, although with smaller dimensions. From the tower the wall ran in a north-easterly direction, but here only the scarp and counter-scarp remained.

This scarp presumably continues under the building known to Christians as the *Cœnaculum*, the traditional scene of the Last Supper ; which also contains the reputed Tomb of David, and is therefore regarded by the Muslims as a sanctuary of especial holiness. Excavation is here impossible ; but Bliss picked up a city wall running along a scarp beyond the Cœnaculum. This wall ran first eastward and then turned abruptly northward, with a tower at the corner ; then eastward again, and then once more northward.

This is clearly a wall which at one time enclosed the Western Hill, running along the western side of the Tyropoeon Valley. It is natural to regard it as a very ancient line of defence, made before the lower reaches of the Tyropoeon Valley had been included in the city area. It might well be in the line of Solomon's rampart, made when he added the Western Hill to the nucleus on the Eastern Hill. Solomon's city must have resembled a capital U with the points directed southward, the Tyropoeon Valley running between the two hills, unoccupied and apparently undefended. But although the scarp, upon which is erected the wall found by Bliss, may very well be part of Solomon's fortification, and may thus indicate to us the city boundary of his time, we cannot identify the wall built on the scarp as Solomon's construction. Fragments of stone with unmistakable Byzantine ornament carved upon them, and building-stones with the characteristic stone-dressing of the Crusader masons, were found incorporated in the structure. There can be no doubt that the wall is a late erection, utilising the Solomonic scarp as a foundation, and erected to enclose the Cœnaculum within the city walls, which had otherwise shrunk to their present exiguous dimensions. The bend in the wall has been reasonably identified with "The Turn in the Wall" referred to in II Chron. xxvi 9. Bliss considers the existing wall to belong to about the middle of the thirteenth century A.D.

We now return to the great rock-scarp from which we began, and which it is generally agreed to identify with the "Tower of the Furnaces" (Nehemiah iii 11). We pass once more to the second tower, whence Bliss turned up the Tyropoeon Valley; and we now learn that this is the meeting-point of two walls. The first of these is that which we have just traced, running along the western side of the Tyropoeon Valley. The second runs along the north side of the Hinnom Valley. It was struck in the course of tunnelling to trace the scarps, and was found to run in a south-easterly direction from the adjacent tower. It ran for 104 feet, at which distance the excavators found a gate. This gate had been repaired four times; corresponding to each repair a new sillstone had been laid down. Most likely this gate is the Valley Gate, or a later representative of the Valley Gate, otherwise called the Harshith Gate: this was the gate at which Jeremiah broke a vessel of pottery as an acted parable of irreparable destruction, and from which Nehemiah issued forth to view at his leisure the ruin of the walls under the clear, cold light of the Syrian moon.

This new wall does not actually impinge on Solomon's corner tower; the width of the fosse cut around the former intervenes. Bliss happily compares the modern citadel of Jerusalem, the moat of which likewise creates a gap in the continuity of the existing wall.

Passing the Valley Gate, we come after a short distance to a tower, where the wall turns slightly, from a south-easterly to an easterly direction. At this point we find evident traces of a reconstruction. We have seen that the Valley Gate has been repaired four times. This tower has been ruined almost to its foundations—three courses only remain—and a second tower in different masonry has been erected over the early masonry, but on a different plan. The upper tower belongs to the wall which we are tracing; the lower tower must therefore be a relic of an earlier wall.

After this tower the wall was traced for some 450 feet, with four projecting towers at irregular intervals; in the middle of this stretch the older wall suddenly appeared again, running quite unconformably with its successor, and presenting two towers. One of these was a bold projection, like those represented by the rock-scarps under the school; the other was a long rectangular structure with a succession of six chambers, side by side, within it. Northward from this remarkable structure, and within the city area, Bliss found the foundations of an immense tower apparently isolated, with walls of unusual thickness. A similar tower was found in the 1924 excavation on the Eastern Hill, but in inferior masonry. No explanation or identification of Bliss's Tower is forthcoming; its purpose and its date are alike unknown. Beneath it were some of the early rock-cut dwellings to which allusion was made above.

From the point at which we have now reached in our study of Bliss's wall, the later wall with which we started disappears, and the tunnels follow the earlier work. As might be expected, this has been much ruined; but it was traced onwards from the tower with six chambers for about 400 feet. There the work had to stop, owing to the remains running under a modern Jewish cemetery. One more tower, much ruined, was found before the wall entered the cemetery. Owing to this vexatious interruption, about 350 feet of the wall had to be left untouched. It was picked up again on the other side of the cemetery, but lost after a run of only 30 feet; the bases cut for the reception of the stones in the underlying rock were uncovered but the stones themselves were gone. The people of Silwan had previously discovered the ancient wall, and had used it as a convenient quarry, removing every stone. Probably had Bliss's work been delayed ten or fifteen years there would not have been a single fragment left for him to discover along the whole length of the Hinnom Valley. After some trials, the wall was once more picked up at what proved to be a small postern gate. Working backward towards the place where the wall had failed, a second gate of small dimensions was found about 80 feet away; beyond this the wall ceased.

The gate first mentioned was guarded by a tower which proved to be at the south-eastern corner of the city. From this tower the wall ran in a north-easterly direction, crossing the embouchure of the Tyropoeon Valley. The constructions revealed here were extremely complicated, and most difficult to unravel. It would appear as though a wall of extra strength had been built here, with external buttresses, which served not only as a city wall, but also as a retaining-wall for the "Old Pool" of Siloam—the reservoir now called El-Birket el-Hamra, which deserves rather closer attention than has yet been paid to it. It is probably by far the oldest of the open reservoirs about Jerusalem. The buttressed wall in spite of its thickness was not strong enough, and it had to be reinforced with additional building on more than one occasion.

We cannot here pause to describe the numerous details of minor topography which were unearthed during the course of the excavation; the streets, drains, cisterns, aqueducts, mosaic pavements, and so forth. Nor can we dwell on the very remarkable little church of Eudoxia built above the Pool of Siloam, architecturally the most interesting of all Bliss's discoveries. For these finds, and for the minor objects discovered during the expedition, reference must be made to Bliss's own account of his work. In this place we must content ourselves with setting forth the most important of his results. This undoubtedly was the determination of the southern boundary of the city at successive periods, including the time of its greatest extension southward.

We have three divisions of the site to take into account: the Eastern Ridge, the slightly crescentic Western Ridge, and the intervening Tyropoeon Valley, with its broad mouth opening into the Kidron. As we have already seen, the Jebusite city was altogether confined to the Eastern Hill. It was the city captured by David, and thenceforth known as his special citadel, David's Fort. Solomon seems to have extended the city over the Western Ridge, but excluding the Tyropoeon Valley. The great rock-scarp under the English School, and the citadel which it must formerly have borne, are most probably part of the work of Solomon, the southern defences of the western half of his city. From this fortress the wall ran along the western side of the Tyropoeon Valley, crossed it at a place where the floor of the valley was raised to a sufficient height to allow this to be done conveniently, and then came down the eastern side, west of the Eastern Hill. The connexion between the two halves of the city to the north must have been very narrow. At the northern end of the eastern division were the Temple and Solomon's Palace. We shall not here describe any of the attempts that have been made to reconstruct these buildings; the descriptions which we possess are totally inadequate as guides for such a restoration. The ideal temple described by Ezekiel is much more easily plotted. That prophet-priest, with his formal mind, probably had a plan in front of him as he wrote; his description reads like an architect's specification. The description of Solomon's Temple in the Book of Kings is more of the nature of an impression. In Solomon's time the "Old Pool" of Siloam was probably already in existence, as a reservoir to collect the winter stream that ran down the Tyropoeon; but it was outside the Jebusite walls, and it remained outside the walls of Solomon.

The line of Solomon's northern wall is not so certainly known; in fact, it must remain for the present a matter of theory. But it was probably determined by an important natural feature, which is still traceable by its influence on the configuration of the modern city, although it is naturally obscured by the accumulation of debris. This is a deep straight valley, tributary to the Tyropoeon, which cuts into the eastern side of the western ridge. Its line is marked by the modern street Suweikat Allun, and by its continuation eastward. The descent of this street by steps, toward the bed of the Tyropoeon, is the modern city's acknowledgment of the existence of this sunken valley. In Solomon's time it must have been a conspicuous rift, and it would have been a natural boundary for a city built at the southern end of the ridge which it intersects. In this case, the modern Hebron, or Jaffa Gate, which stands at the head of this valley, would represent the ancient Corner Gate of the early history of the Kings (*e.g.* II Kings xiv 13), being at the north-west corner of the city as it then was. From this gate the north wall ran eastward, along the south side of the tributary valley, till it abutted on the Temple enclosure. In this northern wall there was a Gate of Ephraim (likewise mentioned in the passage just quoted). The Corner Gate, the Valley Gate, and the Turn of the Wall were all fortified by Uzziah (II Chron. xxvi 9). If we have rightly identified the last-named portion of the wall, it follows that in Uzziah's time the Tyropoeon Valley was still outside the city.

As we read between the lines of the history, subsequent to the death of Solomon, the subordination of Judah to Israel is manifest, although the historian is clearly unwilling to admit it. Consider the story of the battle of Ramoth-Gilead, with which the first book of Kings closes. It is impossible to imagine Ahab saying to a monarch who was wholly independent of him, " I will disguise myself . . . but put thou on thy robes." It is impossible to imagine a wholly independent monarch, especially an Oriental monarch, consenting to act thus as a decoy for arrows intended for the protagonist. Jehoshaphat was quite clearly under orders ; he had to do what his suzerain commanded him to do. Amaziah ventured to challenge the supremacy of Israel, and he received one of the most gallingly contemptuous answers that a king ever got ; but, persisting, he involved his country in war, and the northern fortifications of his capital were demolished (II Kings xiv 8 ff.). When the great king Jeroboam II died, however, the strength of Israel died with him. Internal dissensions and border fighting so weakened the northern kingdom, that the small state of Judah came, in a sense, into its own. Just at the time it was blessed with a series of energetic monarchs —Uzziah, Jotham, and then, after the comparatively futile Ahaz, Hezekiah and Manasseh. To these kings was due the refortification of the city, and also its further extension.

The crucial passage for the determination of the course of the wall in Hezekiah's time is the word of warning in Isaiah xxii. This was uttered by the prophet at some time of civic rejoicing which in his opinion was premature—possibly the averting of the threatened Assyrian siege ; but this question of historical criticism we need not stop to discuss. The special points of importance for us are in vers. 8–11 : "And ye saw the breaches of the City of David that they were many ; and ye gathered together the waters of the Lower Pool. And ye numbered the houses of Jerusalem, and ye brake down the houses to fortify the wall. Ye made also a reservoir between the two walls for the waters of the Lower Pool." The graphic picture of the ramparts allowed to fall into decay, with Oriental *insouciance*, and of the houses of the citizens being feverishly torn down to provide the most easily accessible material for immediate repair in a sudden emergency, is a side-light on ancient Jerusalem life of much value. But especially significant is the reference to an Old Pool, and to a reservoir superseding it, between two walls. As Paton has shown, " Between the Two Walls," a phrase that occurs more than once in the historical and prophetic parts of the Old Testament, must have been an official name for the lower part of the Tyropoeon Valley, which was outside the city, but was bounded by the ramparts of the two ridges. At the lower end of this space is the very ancient reservoir to which allusion has already been made, the Old Pool now called El-Birket el-Hamra. This must always have been outside the walls; the rock-scarp which bore the wall of the Eastern Hill overhangs it; the wall could not have been carried down thence to cross the outside of the pool (the earlier portions of Bliss's wall at this point are probably of Nehemiah's time). This pool seems to have received water from the Virgin's Fountain by some of the earlier conduits, and it was probably used as the source of irrigation of the " King's Gardens " down to the time of Ahaz.

As this pool was outside the city, and could not be otherwise, a second pool was constructed a little higher up. This second pool intercepted the Tyropoeon drainage; in Isaiah's words, it " gathered the waters of the Old Pool." At the same time the last of the numerous conduits from the Virgin's Fountain was cut—the great Siloam Tunnel, by which water still runs from the spring to the pool. This tunnel carried the Virgin's Fountain water into the city. When the Assyrian king would come, he would not find " much water," as Hezekiah had at first feared. The Old Pool, outside the walls, would be dry ; the cave of the Virgin's Fountain would, no doubt, be stopped up ; and a small force could easily prevent a party of the Assyrian army from endeavouring to imitate the feat of Joab by entering the city through the tunnel. They would be hewn down one by one as they emerged from the narrow passage, weary and bedraggled by their long tramp through the water. In modern times, tourists who have rashly adventured to make the passage of the tunnel without adequate protection, have been stopped at both ends of the cutting by a mob of bandits from Silwan, ravenous for *bakhshish*. So much for " Cool Siloam's shady rill " !

The wall of Hezekiah must therefore have run between the two pools, somewhere about the line of the 2109 feet contour, but rising from it eastward after passing the upper pool to abut on the wall of the citadel of the Eastern Hill. Westward it followed the contour-line indicated, as far as the small gate at the corner found by Bliss ; and then it ran along the line traced by him up the Valley of Hinnom.

What is to be said about the *north* wall of these later kings ? This is the most important question of Jerusalem topography. As they built it, so did Nehemiah restore it. As Nehemiah restored it, so did it last, chance local destruction apart, until the days of the Gospel story. If Manasseh left the place where the Church of the Holy Sepulchre now stands *outside* his wall, the claim of that Church to mark the site of the events which it commemorates is admissible, though not necessarily proved. If he included the site, the Church cannot possibly stand in the right place.

It is not easy for a question like this to be discussed with a complete freedom from prepossession. The present writer has already expressed, in this chapter, his total disbelief in any site that has been set up as a rival to the Church of the Holy Sepulchre, and his complete want of sympathy with any attempt to discover such a site. He has personally examined the greater number of the rock-cut tombs that remain open in the hillsides around the city, and he cannot see in the Gospel narratives of the Entombment and the Resurrection anything that would exclude more than a minority of these from the honour of being the actual Holy Sepulchre, although in a large number of cases the probable late date of the tomb would make the identification impossible. There is nothing whatever in the Gospel accounts of the Crucifixion to identify the roadside where the Cross was erected, among the highways radiating from the city. There are, in short, no data whatever to afford us a clue to the identification.

It is a natural impulse for the followers of Christ to wish to express their devotion to Him on the place where He suffered for them ; an impulse so natural that there must be some good in it. It is difficult to feel much patience with those good folk whose uncompromising Protestantism betrays them into the folly of saying piously, "After all, perhaps we are not *meant* to know!" The Father of all Mercies is no obscurantist; we are meant to know everything that it is at all possible to know; it is our duty to use our intellects to the utmost extent of their powers to find out what can be known. *All* knowledge is sacred, and all who seek to advance knowledge are servants of God as well as of Man. If the documents that would guide us are imperfect or destroyed, that is another matter. A mischievous child may tear a page from a parish register-book, and so make it impossible to work out a genealogy. In such a case we regard the occurrence as a mischance, but not necessarily as a Divine interposition. We have no right to suppose that it is any more than a series of such mischances, on a larger scale, that have prevented our working out the infinitely more important problems involved in determining the exact site of the incidents of the Gospel story.

The traditional site is, at the most, not more than half a mile away from the true site. For purposes of devotion, that is quite close enough. But there are serious objections to its claim to stand on the *exact* site. It is necessary to postulate a re-entrant angle in the course of Manasseh's wall for which the relief of the ground affords little justification. We start with two fixed points: the Hebron or Jaffa Gate, and the Damascus Gate, in the masonry of which a much more ancient gate is incorporated, which is evidently of considerable antiquity, and may quite conceivably be the old Fish Gate.

Between these two points there are two possible courses for the wall, the one concave to the outside of the city, the other convex. Fragments of trenches and walls have been found along the *concave* line ; and so far as they go they might be put in as evidence in favour of this alternative. But there are equally imposing fragments that would corroborate the *convex* course ; notably the enigmatical Herodian (?) construction popularly known as "Goliath's Castle," close to the present north-west corner of the city. But even if we assume the re-entrant angle, and the concave line, we meet with the further difficulty that there is no known gate in it, and therefore no probable line of highway crossing it—and this is a necessary concomitant of the site of the Crucifixion. We should also bear in mind what we learnt at Tell es-Safi, that such a re-entrant angle would speedily become filled with noisome rubbish, and would be the last place where a rich man would establish his garden. Owing to the presence of the crowded modern city which covers this debatable ground, it is not likely that it will ever be possible to conduct excavations on a sufficiently extensive scale to settle the question of the course of the north wall.

The Course of Nehemiah's Wall

The little book of Nehemiah is a document of enormous importance. It is a valuable historical record of the beginnings of post-exilic Judaism ; and it is the earliest contemporary account that we possess of the topography of Jerusalem at a definite stage of the city's history. Three chapters are especially valuable in this connexion: the second, containing an account of Nehemiah's night ride around the ruined walls; the third, with a list of the chief builders employed in the reconstruction, and the sections of the wall upon which each gang was engaged; and the twelfth, describing the processions which circled the walls when they were completed, and by which they were dedicated. Incidentally, an interesting parallel might be drawn between this perambulation, and that of the walls of Jericho when they, too, were dedicated—to destruction.

Nehemiah went out by the Valley Gate on his nocturnal reconnaissance. This we have shown is probably the gate found by Bliss in the Hinnom Valley, a little below the Tower of the Furnaces. He rode down the Valley toward the "Dragon's Well." This *must* have been the Virgin's Fountain; even in modern times its intermittent flow is explained as being due to the operations of a great serpent, which periodically drinks up the water. The Valley Gate and the Dragon's Well are named as the two limits of Nehemiah's ride. In travelling from one to the other he passed in turn the Dung Gate, the Fountain Gate, and the King's Pool. At this last point he was obliged to dismount; his "beast," presumably an ass, could not find its way in the semi-darkness through the heaps of ruins. He walked a little way up the "Brook," and, having seen enough of the state of the walls, turned back when he had reached the Virgin's

Fountain, and returned to the Valley Gate. There is no reason to suppose, with some commentators, that he continued his walk round the whole wall ; hampered by an ass that could not pick its steps, he would hardly have done so. The King's Pool is obviously the Upper Pool of Siloam ; the "Brook" is a regular name for the Kidron. Between the Valley Gate and the King's Pool he passed on his way two gates ; and two gates were actually found in this stretch of wall by Bliss.

The features of the wall enumerated in the account of the restoration are twenty-two in number, as under :

1. Sheep Gate.
2. Tower of Hammeah ("the hundred").
3. Tower of Hananel.
4. Fish Gate.
5. Old Gate.
6. Broad Wall.
7. Tower of Furnaces.
8. Valley Gate.
9. Dung Gate.
10. Fountain Gate.
11. Wall of Pool of Shelah.
12. Stairs down from City of David.
13. Sepulchres of David.
14. The Made Pool.
15. House of Mighty Men.
16. Ascent to armoury at turn of wall.
17. Tower standing out at king's house
18. Water Gate.
19. Wall of Ophel.

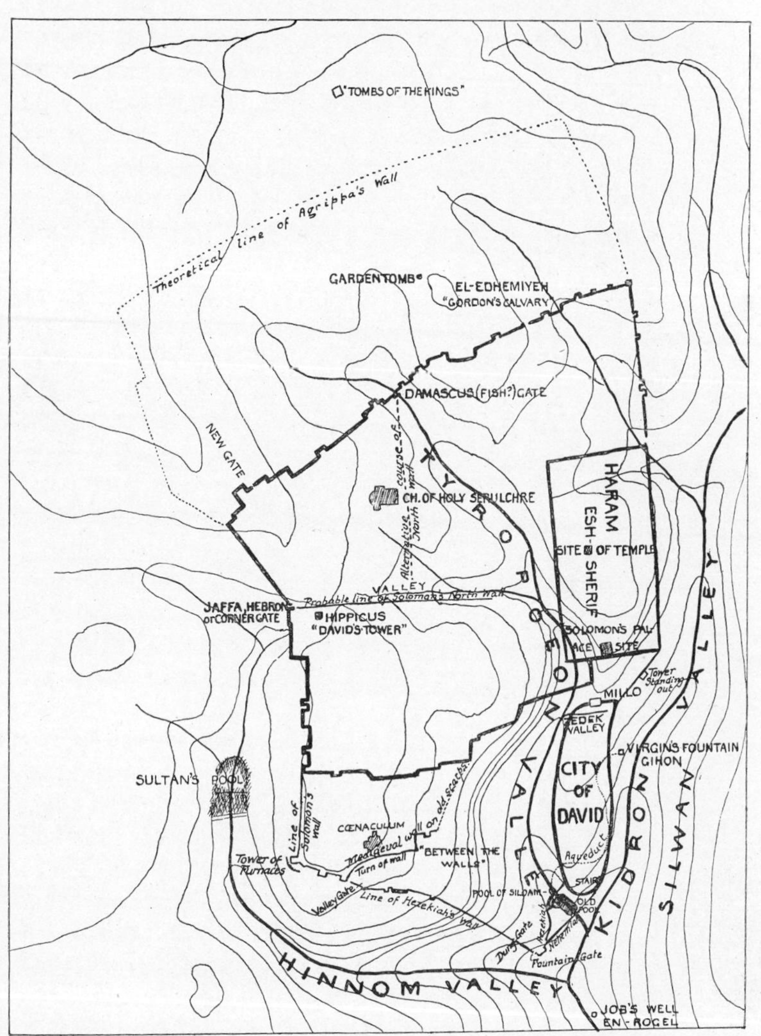
"TOMBS OF THE KINGS"
Theoretical line of Agrippa's Wall
GARDEN TOMB
EL-EDHEMIYEH
"GORDON'S CALVARY"
DAMASCUS (FISH?) GATE
NEW GATE
Alternative course of North wall
CH. OF HOLY SEPULCHRE
TYROPOEON VALLEY
HARAM ESH-SHERIF
SITE OF TEMPLE
Probable line of Solomon's North wall
JAFFA, HEBRON or CORNER GATE
HIPPICUS
"DAVID'S TOWER"
SOLOMON'S PALACE SITE
Tower Standing out
MILLO
ZEDEK VALLEY
VIRGIN'S FOUNTAIN
GIHON
CITY OF DAVID
SULTAN'S POOL
Line of Solomon's wall
CŒNACULUM
Mediaeval wall on old scarps
"BETWEEN THE WALLS"
Aqueduct
Tower of Furnaces
Turn of wall
Valley Gate
Line of Hezekiah's wall
POOL OF SILOAM
STAIRS
OLD POOL
Dung Gate
Hezekiah
Nehemiah
Fountain Gate
KIDRON
SILWAN VALLEY
HINNOM VALLEY
JOB'S WELL
EN-ROGEL

PLAN OF JERUSALEM TO ILLUSTRATE RECENT TOPOGRAPHICAL DISCOVERIES.

20. Horse Gate.
21. East Gate.
22. Ascent to Corner.

The dedicatory procession moved out at the Valley Gate, and there the participants stood facing the new wall. They then divided, one party turning to the right, the other to the left. The first went by the same landmarks, in the same order as in Nehemiah's ride, to the Water Gate; the second by the Tower of the Furnaces round to the Sheep Gate.

We are told that there was a space of 1000 cubits between the Valley Gate and the Dung Gate. Now according to the scale of Bliss's plans, the distance between the two gates which we have taken as representing these openings, measured along the face of the wall with all its windings, is 1840 feet. We must remember that 1000 cubits is merely a round number, and therefore need not be taken as more than approximately accurate; reckoning the cubit at 20·51 inches, this would be a length of slightly over 1709 feet, which is close enough to the actual dimension. We may therefore safely identify the Valley Gate with the gate a short distance down the lowest reach of the Hinnom Valley; the Dung Gate with the small gate near the corner; the Fountain Gate—no doubt so called from its proximity to Job's Well—with the gate in the corner tower. The Wall of the Pool of Shelah, that is of Shiloah, is doubtless the thick buttressed wall that Bliss found, including—now for the first time—the Old Pool within the walls. The perished with him. The Corner Tower is unknown. The purpose of this wall was to enclose the till then unprotected suburb of Bezetha, which had grown up outside the Old Wall. Now Bezetha is usually identified with the quarter of the modern city north of the Haram area, within the present wall. There is no evidence on the existing surface of the ground that there were any closely-packed city buildings outside the present north wall. It is indeed improbable ; a wall such as must be postulated if we are to make it run beside the " Tombs of the Kings " would include in the area the inconvenient hill El-Edhemiyeh (" Gordon's Calvary "). It is not impossible that the " Sepulchral Cavern of the Kings " is the great quarry-cave now called " Solomon's Quarries " ; if so, then Agrippa's Wall *must* follow the line of the present north wall, and the other landmarks must be sought for along its course.

But the problem is complicated by certain structures which were still extant in April 1838, when they were observed by Robinson, and were reported upon by him with lamentable superficiality. They must have been totally destroyed, probably by masons in search of stone, soon after Robinson's time, for no one seems ever to have verified his all too brief description. In Robinson's time the land north of the city was quite free from modern buildings ; now it is thickly covered with public and private establishments, and any attempt to check his observations by excavation would be impossible. He describes them as " foundations consisting of

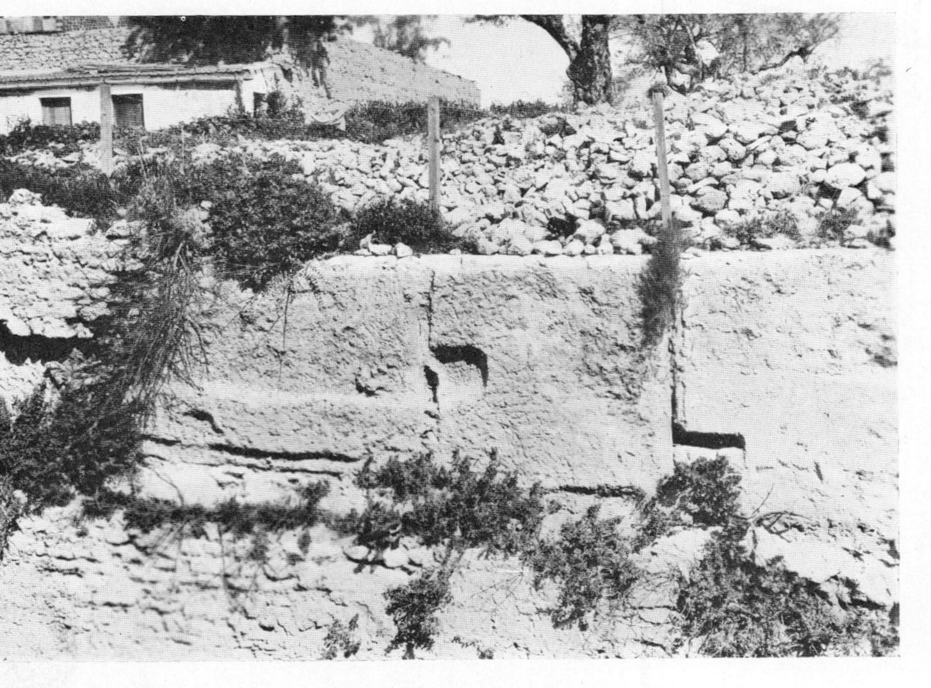

LARGE STONES NORTH OF DAMASCUS GATE, JERUSALEM.

large hewn blocks of stone, of a character corresponding to the works of those ages"—*i.e.* to the time of Agrippa: and he relates how he traced them from a point west by north of the present north-west corner of the city walls, and 700 feet away from it, and followed them in detached fragments zigzagging over the ground, and ending near the "Tombs of the Kings." In the side of a now open and ruined cistern, east of the road running north from the Damascus Gate, there are three very large stones end to end, which must form part of some imposing building of the Herodian period; but the evidence is insufficient to permit us to assert definitely that they belong to a city wall. If the fragments of wall seen by Robinson were really those of Agrippa's wall, the opportunity of verifying this has gone by for ever; and, it must be added, the very foundations of the houses that it presumably enclosed have also disappeared, with the potsherds and other relics of occupation which ought to strew the area which Agrippa by this hypothesis added to the city.

In the vast majority of cases, both inside and outside the Holy Land, the determination by excavation or otherwise, of the *exact* site where any event took place is a perfectly hopeless task. Only a very limited number of transactions could possibly leave a permanent impression upon the place where they were performed. A Paul may preach on Mars' Hill; but no one could point out, twenty-four hours later, where he had stood, unless an eye-witness should give spoken or written testimony on the matter.

have been taught; to the Church of the Ascension; and to numerous other sites of the kind. Of these we can say no more than that they have been arbitrarily selected from among a large number of possible competitors.

There is a fourth class; the sites of which no reasonable doubt can exist. What are these?

In the first place, we may take it that the chief natural features are definitely determined. There can be no doubt about the identification of the Mount of Olives; of the Kidron, Tyropoeon, and Hinnom Valleys—an attempt was once made to identify the Hinnom Valley with El-Wad (the modern name of the valley here called the Tyropoeon), but it only caused confusion without any compensating advantage—and of the water-sources Gihon (the Virgin's Fountain) and En-Rogel (Job's Well). The identification of Gihon with any of the Herodian or Saracenic reservoirs to the west of the city is now quite abandoned.

Secondly, we now know definitely that the Jebusite city was on the Eastern Ridge, and that it was in all probability Solomon who extended the city to cover the Western Ridge. The site of the Solomon's Temple was certainly that now covered by the Haram esh-Sherif.

The modern Pool of Siloam is certainly that constructed by Hezekiah and referred to in John ix 7, although it is now very much smaller than it originally was. The tunnel connecting this pool with the Virgin's Fountain, likewise, is unquestionably that made by Hezekiah in anticipation of the Assyrian siege. But, on the contrary, it is certain that the village of Silwan, on the opposite side of the Kidron, is *not* the Biblical Siloam, although it bears its name. The rock underlying this village is honeycombed with ancient tombs, and no Hebrew community would have established itself in a place so unclean. There is no *tell* or other evidence of ancient occupation underlying the modern houses of the village. Probably the Biblical Shiloah, Siloam, was a district of Jerusalem itself, perhaps the low-lying land at the embouchure of the Tyropoeon Valley.

The line of the southern half of the city as it was in the days of Solomon, of the later monarchy, of Nehemiah, and of the Crusades, is known ; but there are several points of detail that remain to be cleared up by more extensive excavation than has yet been carried out.

This is the full tale of Old Testament sites about which we can be sure in Jerusalem and its neighbourhood. When we come to consider the sites of the Gospels, we are confronted at every step with ambiguities and impossibilities. The use of caves as stables is quite common in Palestine ; but there is not the slightest evidence that the Nativity took place in a stable. The Child, *after His birth*, was laid in a manger, because there was no room in the inn ; but the story of the visit of the Wise Men represents the Epiphany as taking place *in a house*. Notwithstanding the antiquity of the noble and venerable Church of the Holy Nativity at Bethlehem, we cannot accept the caves underneath its floor as being any more authentic than the three of its sides; a single pillar standing in the middle of each of the long sides, dividing the face of the colonnade in two, made, with the single opening at one of the narrow sides, the five "porches" under which the sick folk lay. The fourth side, we gather, was not covered with a portico. Then we learn that it was "by the sheep . . ." Most unfortunately the substantive qualified by the adjective has dropped out. Grammatical concord shows that it must have been a feminine word, and it is natural to think of the Sheep-*Gate*, which, as we have seen, was in the north of the city. A variant form of the name "Bethesda" which some MSS. preserve, namely "Bethzatha," recalls *Bezetha*, the name of the northern quarter of the city.

Three great reservoirs in the region indicated have been fixed upon at different times as being the pool in question. One is the pair of "Twin Pools" under the Castle of Antonia. Another is the large reservoir called Birket Israin, north of the Haram—once an important water-store, and now filled with rubbish. The third is the immense cistern in front of the Crusaders' beautiful Church of St. Anne, near the gate of St. Stephen. The first of these was shown to the Bordeaux Pilgrim as Bethesda (he calls it Bethsaida). The third was identified therewith at least as early as the Crusades; for the site of a Church, or rather, of several superposed churches, has been exposed by the White Fathers who are in charge of St. Anne's. The architectural history of these structures is desperately difficult to decipher from the extant remains. Relics of a tempera painting were visible in a niche in these ruins, down to the time of the war, when they were almost completely destroyed; the painting represented the angel troubling the water. There is a good copy of this painting in the library of the Palestine Exploration Fund. Birket Israin was the Bethesda of popular tradition till the pool at St. Anne's was reopened: the latter is now the generally accepted site.

But notwithstanding this testimony to the antiquity of the tradition, it is very difficult to see how events, such as are described in the Gospel narrative, could have taken place here. There is nothing in any of these cisterns, so far as we can see, to account for the story of the troubling of the waters. There are arches and vaultings, but nothing that can fairly be called "porches" surrounding any of the cisterns; although it is only fair to say that much excavation has still to be done at St. Anne's, and it is impossible to predict what future work may reveal. But the reservoir itself is a forbidding pit with vertical sides, about 15 or 20 feet deep (on this point I speak from memory, and cannot give the figure accurately); sick folk who rashly flung themselves into the water, in their haste to secure precedence, would run very serious risk of being drowned, rather than cured of whatever malady they may have been suffering.

Although the sentence about the troubling of the water has not quite such good MS. authority as the rest of the narrative, it is almost required to explain the story. Something happened at in these running waters, wherein dogs and swine have been cast night and day, and hast washed and wiped the outer skin—which harlots and flute-girls anoint and wash and wipe and beautify for the lust of men, but inwardly they are filled with scorpions and all wickedness. But I and My disciples, who, thou sayest, have not bathed, we have bathed in the waters of Everlasting Life which come from the . . ."

Here the fragment breaks off.

The writer was not well informed as to the topography of the Temple. We know nothing from other sources of a specially holy "Place of Purification." Nor does the expression "Pool of David" occur elsewhere. But yet the narrative does not read wholly like an invention. A Pool ascribed to an ancient king of Jerusalem, with *running* water, used for purifications—the reference to dogs and swine is hardly to be taken literally, but may well refer to the spiritually unclean *men* who there sought outward cleansing; indeed the narrative in John v makes it clear that the man whose healing is there recorded was bearing in his disease the penalty of an evil life—all these indications suit the Pool of Siloam *and no other* pool known to us. While we cannot lay too much stress on this papyrus fragment in matters of detail, it is interesting to notice the reference to steps leading down to the water and up again. Such steps would greatly facilitate the use of the pool as a bathing-place by the sick who frequented it.

Note.—As these sheets are passing through the press, the discovery of walls identified with Agrippa's North Wall is announced: but no particulars have yet come to hand.

CHAPTER III

EXCAVATION AND POLITICAL HISTORY

THE chief light shed by excavation upon Palestinian political history has come, not from Palestine itself, but from foreign countries which from time to time influenced it in one way or another.

In documents dating from the fifth millennium B.C. Elamite kings claim to have extended their authority as far as the " Great Western Sea," which can only mean the Mediterranean. This would imply that they included Syria at least, if not Palestine, under their sway. But as yet no trace whatever of these ancient monarchs has been found upon Palestinian soil. Letters from the cities of Canaan, discovered in the archive-chamber of the Heretic King at Tell el-Amarna, are eloquent on the matter of marauders which they call " Sutu " and " Khabiru "; but these peoples would have had no existence for us if we were dependent for our historical knowledge upon the results of excavations in Palestine alone. A little later, an Egyptian envoy called Wen-Amon suffers many things at the hands of an evidently powerful and prosperous people called Zakkala, settled on the sea-coast from the town of Dor northwards to Phœnicia; but so far as any relic of these Zakkala on their ancient heritage is concerned, this people has vanished like the snow of bygone years. Nowhere in the whole country can we trace the faintest footprint of Abraham, Isaac, Jacob; of Samuel, Saul, David, Isaiah. It is a Moabite king who tells us of the greatness of the seemingly insignificant Omri. Kings of Assyria tell us, on the other hand, of the littleness of Jehu and of Hezekiah; for they treat them as mere *roitelets*, no better than others whose doings they relate, but of whom we never heard before—Sharludari, Yamani, Padi, Aziru, and the rest. Even when an engineering work of considerable extent, such as the Siloam Tunnel, is undertaken, the king under whose auspices it is carried out omits to record his connexion with it. One of the workmen, it is true, scribbles on the wall for our instruction a record of the way in which the tunnel was excavated; but he enters into no historical details. A person describing himself as "Servant of Azariah," not improbably the great King Uzziah, loses a seal at Jerusalem; another, calling himself "Servant of Jeroboam," not improbably King Jeroboam II, leaves his seal behind at Megiddo. But otherwise the procession of the kings of Judah and Israel have passed, and have left no more impression than the shadows projected on a moving-picture screen. We possess the foundations of Nehemiah's walls: but Ezra might never have stood on his "pulpit of wood" for all the light that excavation has thrown upon him. The veil of silence is still draped over the mysterious fate of Zerubbabel, who vanishes so abruptly from the stage on which he seemed destined to play a leading part. Ben-Sira's words of wisdom are stilled in the unknown site of his school. The rich gifts which Aristeas is alleged to have carried from Ptolemy Philadelphus to the High Priest at Jerusalem have not yet rewarded the excavator. Apart from the records of historians, and coins, the terrible Antiochus might never have been heard of, had not a *mauvais sujet* been moved to the obscure witticism of caricaturing some one of his name as a giraffe, on a small stone tablet found at Gezer ; nor would his enemies, the family of the Maccabees, have had any better fate, had not one Pampras, dwelling in the same city, scratched a spiteful curse against Simon on a fragment of limestone. We possess one of the notices warning strangers from trespassing upon the inner court of Herod's Temple. We have the tomb-inscription of Nicanor of Alexandria, who made or presented the " Beautiful Gate " of the Temple. But Herod and Pilate, Annas and Caiaphas, Nicodemus and Gamaliel, exist for us only in the Books that tell us of them. A recent discovery has thrown some light upon the foundation of the synagogue of the Libertines, whose leaders were among the bitterest accusers of the protomartyr Stephen. But it tells us of people called Theodotos, Vettenos, Simonides, whose names are quite new to us. It might almost be thought, on a superficial view of the results of excavation, that the excavator and the historian were working in totally different fields.

Now, if some pre-exilic king—say Solomon, whose polytheism was notorious—had erected a monument in which he ascribed some of his glory to Dodah, or Ishum, or to any other of the deities whose names are thus recorded for us, there can be no question that in a time of purer worship even the great name of Solomon would not have saved such a monument from destruction. And iconoclasm of the kind, once begun, would continue quite automatically and unreasoningly. The mere fact that an inscription was in the Old Hebrew character would be sufficient to condemn it to destruction at the hands of some fanatic, who might possibly be unable to read it. The violent actions and reactions between Paganism and Yahwism, in the centuries intervening between the return from the Captivity and the destruction of Jerusalem under Titus, would certainly involve in ruin records that named any god other than Him with whom Moses and Samuel had covenanted in the name of the nation.

Compared with Syria, Palestine is ill-watered and unfertile. Of the two provinces, the former would certainly have been the first to be settled and civilised. On the other hand, owing to its superior attractiveness, Syria would be more liable to the strain of foreign aggression and foreign conquest.

In Palestine, no trace of settled human occupation has hitherto been found, dating further back than about 3000 B.C. In making this statement, it is not forgotten that Palæolithic implements have been found in considerable numbers, testifying to an occupation many thousands of years earlier. But the nomadic hunters of the Palæolithic age can hardly be described as " settled "; and nothing has yet been found to bridge the gap between them and the late Neolithic folk. We do not go so far as to say that the country was uninhabited, what time the Elamite kings, if we may believe their word, were lording it to the confines of the Great Western Sea; but such inhabitants as it had must have been of a civilisation so low that they have left behind no recognisable traces.

Naturally we can say nothing of the political organisation and connexions of a people so evanescent. We can imagine them dwelling in goat-skin tents, huddled together around the various springs of water. Sunk in the depths of poverty, they aroused no cupidity: they were in what a popular proverb declares to be the happy state of having no history. They were a simple, uncivilised, non-Semitic race who minded their own humble affairs. Perhaps no one even thought it worth his while to oppress them, although in the ancient East, whatever may be the case in the East of to-day, every one was either oppressed or an oppressor. When we come into direct contact with them, at Gezer, we find them dwelling in caves, manufacturing very rude pottery and flint knives, and burning their dead, unlike most Neolithic people and all Semites.

There is no collective name by which to call this Neolithic people. The Old Testament record gives us hints of traditions about ancient told us little or nothing about their internal or external personal relations. The Tell el-Amarna tablets still remain our chief authority on this subject. They reveal a complete lack of cohesion between the various city-states. Each acts for itself; just as, in the Book of Joshua, the Gibeonites consult their own safety, and fly for refuge to the invader when their brethren take vengeance upon them for their treachery. Each city has its own governor, who grandiloquently describes himself as its "king." Each king exercises independently the right of direct access to the Egyptian suzerain. Between the cities there is envy, hatred, and malice *in excelsis*. Much the same might be said of the villages in modern Palestine, which represent these ancient cities in site, often in name, and in the external appearance of the houses and of their inhabitants. What happened in A.D. 1903 was only a modern picture of what was happening fourteen centuries B.C. among those troublesome subjects of the unhappy dreamer of Tell el-Amarna. In that year there was a most serious cattle-plague, which had the ultimate effect of permanently doubling the cost of living, so great was the destruction wrought in the herds. It might have been checked at the outset; but it was artificially propagated over the entire country. For, as the cattle of each village in its turn was affected, the inhabitants said one to the other: Why should we lose our cattle, and those of this village or that in the neighbourhood preserve theirs? Why should they gain by our loss? In the face of this childish spiteful jealousy all economic considerations were thrown to the winds ; plague-stricken cattle were secretly driven to the pastures of the sound cattle ; and the murrain was thus handed on from village to village, with most disastrous consequences to the country at large. In like manner, a woman in one of the Palestinian towns, who had lost a child through scarlatina, sent another child infected with the disease to play in the streets and to spread the infection. Why, she asked, should I lose my child and the other women keep theirs ? Onc who has been an eyewitness of such acts in modern times will feel no surprise at the petty squabbles and the childish tale-bearing of city against city in the time of Akhnaton, suicidal though such disunion was in the presence of the advancing Aramæans.

The Tell el-Amarna letters are, on the whole, dreary reading, notwithstanding their supreme interest and value. There is a mechanical monotony in their diction which is perfectly extraordinary ; if all these kinglets had agreed to chorus the same thing in the ear of their nominal master, there would not have been a more perfect accord. The jargon of diplomacy, especially when it is carried on in a language not native to the writer, has a tendency to fall into stereotyped formulæ : if we set ourselves to read through an edition of these letters we find the majority to be cast into some such form as this—" To my lord, I A. B., king of C. D. Seven times do I prostrate myself on breast and back." Then follows a rigmarole of compliments and flattery which wastes several lines of precious space, and then the writer proceeds to business. "The Sutu, or the Khabiru, or some other enemy, is pressing on my city. Let the king send me assistance for I am ever loyal to the king's majesty. Y. Z. is conspiring against the king, and is giving help to the enemy; but as for me," etc., etc. We look up the letters of Y. Z. and we find, without surprise, that he makes countercharges against A. B., and speaks in a tone of injured innocence about the charges that have been made against himself. The professions which both writers alike make before the Egyptian king are pitifully hollow: in current phrase, no one would hang a decent dog on the evidence of any of these Canaanite kings. It is unlikely that the king of Egypt was really verdant enough to be imposed upon by any of them: at least, so far as we can find, he usually left their letters unanswered.

What we now want, and may some time hope to obtain, is a similar collection, of equal extent, of letters between the Canaanite kings themselves. We know what Abd-Khiba king of Jerusalem said to the king of Egypt about Shuwardata king of Keilah. We know what Shuwardata said about Abd-Khiba. To complete the picture we require the private correspondence of Abd-Khiba with Shuwardata. Were these two worthies in league, denouncing each other as a blind? The archive-chamber of one of the local kings, whenever it may be found, may be expected to deepen the lurid colours with which the Tell el-Amarna letters paint the Canaan of their time. It is to be feared that much of this internal correspondence may have been conducted on papyrus, and therefore has perished; the Babylonian *lingua franca* would naturally be used chiefly in communicating with the foreigner. Still, some tablets have been found at Taanach, which are just of the kind that are desiderated. These are part of the correspondence of Ishtar-Washur, king of Taanach; they are as yet the only important group of tablets of this nature. The Lachish tablet is hard to understand, the Gezer Babylonian tablet is a mere fragment. There is but little in common between the Taanach and the Amarna tablets, though they undoubtedly belong to the same period. One of them is a list of names, quite possible a catalogue of conspirators; among these we find mention of one Tagu, a person who appears several times in the Amarna correspondence as a suspect. He was the father-in-law of the noted bandit Milkili, and a partner with him in his depredations. We find Ishtar-Washur collecting money from one correspondent, and making arrangements about arms, tools, and store of wine with another: and although we have only detached items from his postbag, they are enough to involve his proceedings in deep suspicion.

It must be freely admitted that the result of excavation has been to confuse rather than to illuminate the history of Palestine from the Tell el-Amarna period down to, let us say, the time of Samuel. This is by no means an argument against excavation. It is only a proof that we have not yet succeeded in collecting all the parts of the puzzle. In time they *must* all fit together and make a complete picture. If we do not succeed in this task, it is our own fault ; we are by no means in the position of the unhappy victim whose friend presented her with a dissected picture puzzle into which she had mixed a handful of pieces from another set. History and archæology play no such despicable practical jokes. Even when an excavator finds a sixteenth-century German token inside a third-century Palestinian tomb (as has happened) a simple explanation of the intrusion is forthcoming. As a result of the excavations that have been made in Palestine and elsewhere, we see at present a series of mountain peaks. These rise above a sea of impenetrable mist. We cannot yet discern how they are connected together ; we cannot with certainty map the valleys underneath. In time we shall be able to do this ; and we shall wonder at our blindness in missing the very simple solution that will present itself.

These remarks are especially applicable to what is one of the darkest problems of the early Biblical history—the date of the Exodus, and the relations of the immigrant tribes of Israel to Egypt on the one hand, and to Canaan on the other. There are admittedly most difficult critical problems within the Pentateuchal record of the Exodus and the immigration into Canaan, but the main lines of the story are perfectly clear. A community which had formerly enjoyed favour is reduced to servitude by an Egyptian king. Their oppressor dies ; his successor continues his policy. The community escapes under a divinely ordained leader ; their oppressor and his host, pursuing them, are drowned in the Red Sea. After many adventures they reach the Land of Promise; partially carry out their "marching orders" to exterminate the existing inhabitants, and establish themselves in their stead. One of the cities which they had built, under the lash of their oppressor's taskmasters, was called Rameses; it was therefore natural to identify the Pharaoh of the Oppression with the mighty monarch Rameses (Ramessu) II, and the Pharaoh of the Exodus with his son and successor Merneptah. The chronology of the succeeding periods carried through until we reach fixed dates in the time of Solomon, is not very conclusive, but it accords fairly well with the dating thus indicated for the Exodus.

It must be admitted that the effect of excavation has been to add most bewildering complications to this simple story; and it is now quite clear that the course of the Hebrew colonisation of Palestine must have been a much more gradual and elaborate process. The first discovery which indicated this conclusion was that of the mummy of Merneptah himself, concealed in the tomb of Amon-Hotep II. Whatever explanation we may choose to adopt of the story of the crossing of the Red Sea, it is mere casuistry to pretend that it does not imply that Pharaoh was drowned there along with his host; this may not be actually narrated in so many words, but it is quite clearly presupposed.

Next came the great "victory" stele of Merneptah, giving another severe blow to the traditional explanation of the Exodus narrative.

This monument bears a pæan celebrating the exploits of the king, and it ends with remarkable words to the effect that Ashkelon, Gezer, and Janoam are destroyed, and *Israel is wasted and hath no seed.* So that Israel was already the name of a settled agricultural community in Palestine when Merneptah caused this monument to be erected. A small object bearing the name of Merneptah, which has been explained as a portable sundial, was actually found at Gezer.

The Beisan stelæ add further difficulties. Seti I describes how he accepted an invitation from the king of Beth-Shean to assist him against the Hittite lord of Hamath, and how in a single day he gained the victory. So that Egyptian kings could and did conduct important and successful expeditions into the Promised Land at a time not far removed from the traditional date of the Exodus. Ramessu II then sets up a stele in the same place, extolling himself after his manner. It is said that most of the inscription consists of jejune boasting, but that there is one sentence, which, if the translation is verified, will be of great importance—the statement that he built the city of "Rameses" with Semitic labourers. This would certainly be a startling confirmation of the story of the Israelite oppression in Egypt; but how then are we to reconcile it with the evidence already set forth from the monuments of Merneptah? Later still, Ramessu III is still strong enough in Palestine to set up a statue of himself in this important town. If these Egyptian kings were thus

STELE OF RAMESSU II, FOUND AT BETH-SHEAN.

influential enough to erect fortresses and to set up monuments of themselves in a town at the very heart of Palestine, how could the Israelite slaves expect to escape from Egyptian domination by transferring themselves thither ?

The Tell el-Amarna letters come down to us from some two hundred years before the generally received date for the Exodus. On certain of these we read of raiders called Khabiru, who are menacing the Canaanite cities. If letters, written at the time of the Hebrew campaign under Joshua, had reached us from Jericho or from Ai, the writers would have spoken of the Hebrews in just the same way as Abd-Khiba and his contemporaries speak of the Khabiru and the Sutu. The two names, Hebrew, Khabiru, are practically identical ; the coincidence of name, if it be a mere coincidence, is perfectly extraordinary. But, on the other hand, there is a complete lack of any coincidence of detail. If we had lost the Book of Joshua, we could not recover its narrative from the Amarna letters. Thus, where both narratives name kings of specific towns, their names are quite different in the two documents.

Moreover, to add yet one more embarrassing complication, the tablets recently discovered at Boghaz-köi, the site of Khattushash, capital of the Hittite Empire, reveal to us marauding Khabiru at work there, as well as in Southern Palestine.

There is a third possibility remaining, which would transfer the historical events that underlie the narrative of the Exodus back to a date yet more remote. Early in the second millennium B.C. Egypt had been groaning under a foreign domination, a succession of piratical Semites, whom Manetho has taught us to call the *Hyksos*. These shepherd-chieftains left a long-lasting legacy of hatred in the country over which they had tyrannised ; there is an echo of it in the Book of Genesis, where we read that *shepherds are an abomination to the Egyptians*. The chronology of the Hyksos period is very difficult to unravel ; but their expulsion may be dated some three hundred years before the time of the Tell el-Amarna tablets. It has been suggested that the story of the Exodus is the reverse picture, from the Hyksos point of view, of the expulsion of these foreigners. But it is difficult to see how the subsequent events can possibly be reconciled with one another on this theory. A couple of centuries after the expulsion of the Hyksos, Tahutmes III made the great expedition in which he practically subdued Palestine to himself, and established the Egyptian empire in Asia which Akhnaton was destined to fritter away. True, in the lists of places conquered by Tahutmes, there are names which can be written, in the conventional manner of the English Biblical translation, Joseph-el and Jacob-el ; but it is really impossible to say what this fact means, and what bearing it has upon the criticism of the Patriarchal traditions on the one hand, and of the Exodus narrative on the other. One of the Hyksos kings had a name that looks like the Semitic name Jacob, but this also may possibly be nothing more than a mere coincidence.

To sum up, we have three possible correlations of the Exodus story with historical events, which excavation in Egypt has revealed to us; but all three are involved in difficulties through which without further light it will be impossible to see our way. If we take the Hyksos expulsion as representing the Exodus, we shall find it impossible to explain the condition of things which exist in the Tell el-Amarna period, with any conservation of the Biblical story whatsoever. If we choose the Amarna period as being the time of the Exodus, the details will be found quite irreconcileable, although the broad outlines are not dissimilar. If we return to the old theory of Ramessu II and Merneptah, we must explain the "Israel" stele of Merneptah in some more satisfactory way than has yet been discovered, and we must also explain how the Israelites hoped to get away from the sway of an oppressor who maintained a great fortress in the middle of the land to which they were fleeing.

Another unexpected fact has been revealed by the Amarna letters. From the Biblical account we should have gathered that between the Israelites and the Canaanites there was a great gulf fixed, in language, in theology, and in general morality. But now we know that there was singularly little difference between the two peoples. The Canaanites spoke a language scarcely to be distinguished from Hebrew. When the Israelites entered Canaan, they came to no foreign land; they settled among their blood brothers, served their gods, and spoke their speech.

In short, there is no section of the Biblical history upon which fresh light is more urgently needed than on this period of the beginning of the Israelite occupation.

It can hardly be said that the fascinating but very difficult history of the Judges has had much light thrown upon it from excavation, save in the nature of sidelights upon certain details. The problem of the Philistines, their origin and civilisation, remains much where it was before Palestine excavation began. There is now known to have been a strong Ægean influence on the culture of Palestine just at the time when the Philistines were at the height of their power. This to a great extent supersedes the Egyptian influence which is equally prominent in the strata corresponding to the preceding centuries. But some of the latest students are questioning—perhaps with undue scepticism—the confident ascription of certain forms of pottery to the Philistines. Here, once more, we need further light.

Some day a happy explorer may have the good fortune to find an inscription, or a collection of tablets, written in the " speech of Ashdod," which lingered in the country down to the time of Nehemiah, although that uncompromising advocate of racial purity does not seem to have appreciated the high privilege which he enjoyed in hearing it spoken.

But although we cannot yet listen to the words of the triumph-songs that the Philistines sang over their great enemy brought low, we can wield the ox-goad of Shamgar and the dagger of

Ehud; at least, we can form an idea of what these primitive weapons looked like. In the company of the latter we can flee past the Standing Stones, and we shall not mistake them, as pre-excavation translators of the Old Testament have done, for "quarries" or "images." We can thresh wheat in a hidden winepress with Gideon; although I fear that it is not without a twinge of unregenerate regret that we watch him perpetrating the vandalism of destroying that remarkably complete and interesting High Place. Perhaps a time may come when we shall be able to sit down with Gaal's drunken followers in the Temple of Shechem, and curse Abimelech—that is, if we care to adventure ourselves in such disreputable company. [The discovery of one or two of the pre-Solomonic Temples of Palestine (other than High Places) is greatly to be desired.] We can handle the "riding-stone" of the mill, with which the unknown benefactress of Thebez rid the world of that same Abimelech. We can read the dark story of Jephthah without feeling obliged to cast about for far-fetched loopholes of escape from its literal truthfulness; for we have now learnt from excavation that Jephthah and his contemporaries had not advanced beyond the conception of a deity who, upon occasion, called for human sacrifices. In general, we can paint in its true colours the drab background of the stage on which were played out the sordid tragedy of the mighty Samson, the pitiful tragi-comedy of Micah and his private oratory, and the gruesome episode, hardly to be matched in the records of the most degraded of savages, of the Levite of Bethlehem and his concubine. The contents of the strata of accumulation indicate that at this time there was a sudden collapse of Palestinian culture. Never very high, it had attained to a respectable elevation just before. But now it does not decline; it smashes. As a result of the Israelite settlement in Canaan, the civilisation of the country, such as it was, was effaced, and had to be painfully built up again with the help of the cultured Philistines.

Excavation has been begun under Danish auspices at Seilun, the site of Shiloh. It is as yet far too early to say anything of its results; there, if anywhere, we might hope for light on the personality of Eli, who appears so abruptly on the scene; and on the architecture of that earliest of Hebrew temples—for it was certainly not a tent—in which the youthful Samuel had his vision of Divine judgment. We have not yet found a statue of Dagon; and Beth-Shemesh has been dug without revealing a hoof-print of the cattle that brought back the Ark. We are still ignorant of who the mysterious Jeconiah may have been, whose sons held themselves sulkily aloof from the village rejoicing at the return of the sacred emblem, thereby bringing the Divine wrath upon the community. This curious episode is recorded in the Septuagint version only.

It would be unfair to demand from excavation the "verification" or even the elucidation of incidents such as these. They pass and leave no more permanent trace on the surface of the earth than will the heavy shower of rain that is falling as I write these words. They survive only in the memories of eye-witnesses and of those to whom eye-witnesses report them, by speech or by writing. Obviously no amount of excavation, however meticulously watched and reported, could either verify or amplify a narrative like this.

But if we turn a page or two, we shall find an excellent illustration of how excavation helps in the solution of seemingly insoluble difficulties. We may describe it here, as the subject of the bearing of excavation on the written record has just now come under our notice; although it would perhaps be more appropriate to the following chapter than to that which the reader is now perusing.

In I Samuel xiii 19–22 we find the following passage, which we quote from the Revised Version:

> "Now there was no smith found throughout all the land of Israel; for the Philistines said, Lest the Hebrews make them swords or spears. But all the Israelites went down to the Philistines, to sharpen every man his share, and his coulter, and his axe, and his mattock: yet they had a file for the mattocks, and for the coulters, and for the forks, and for the axes, and to set the goads. So it came to pass, in the day of battle, that there was neither sword nor spear found in the hand of any of the people, but with Saul and with Jonathan his son was there found."

The general sense of this passage is plain enough. The Philistines were at the time in complete domination over the people of Israel. As a modern Power prevents gun-running among subject communities, so the Philistines prevented their Israelite vassals from becoming possessed of "up-to-date" weapons. Now, excavation has shown that just about the time of David bronze was giving place to iron as the principal material from which weapons and implements were made; and this paragraph evidently refers to such a stage in civilisation. The Israelites were not yet out of the bronze-age culture; even a generation or two later it was thought wrong to use the newly introduced metal, iron, in erecting a sacred building (II Kings vi 7). But the more advanced Philistines were already acquainted with the use and technique of iron, and their position on the sea-coast enabled them to command the trade in this commodity, and to restrict its extension into the Hebrew *Hinterland*. The Hebrews were permitted to purchase agricultural tools of iron; but so absolute was the control of the Philistines, that they were able to prevent any one of the Hebrews from acquiring and exercising the art of the smith, lest he should reverse the prophet's dream of the millennium, and beat these instruments of peaceful craft into artillery of war. It was actually noticed, in the Gezer excavation, that agricultural implements of iron appeared a little sooner than military weapons of the same material. The late Andrew Lang observed the same succession in the Homeric civilisation. In consequence of this lack of native smiths, all the Israelite owners of agricultural tools of iron were obliged to go down " to [the land of] the Philistines "—the bracketed words preserved by the Greek version have been accidentally dropped in the Hebrew—in order to have them sharpened and set whenever necessity for this process should arise. Only the king and his heir-apparent, by their superior wealth and influence, were in a position to break the embargo. They had iron swords or spears; their followers had either their primitive bronze weapons, or else a heterogeneous assemblage of agricultural tools snatched up and adapted as improvised instruments of attack.

So much for the general sense of the passage. But when we come to consider it in detail, the difficulties multiply. There are some obvious corruptions. We have already noted one, the omission of the words " the land of " in the Hebrew text. The scribe who wrote the parent manuscript, from which all extant MSS. of the Hebrew text are descended, was probably rather sleepy when he was transcribing this paragraph. In the first list of implements, he has dropped out the name of the *fourth*, and repeated the name of the *first* in its place; but this error we can correct with the aid of the repetition of the list. The real difficulties lie in the next verse. This originally began with another passage now lost from the Hebrew: " And the harvest was ready for reaping "—just the time when the furbishing up of agricultural tools would be necessary. Contrariwise, the next passage is lost from the Greek, but preserved by the Hebrew. though in an imperfect form. The reason for these defects was one of the commonest sources of error in copying—the two consecutive sentences had each a prominent word, and the two words much resembled one another in external appearance, so that the scribe's eye overlooked the one and fastened on the other. As the second sentence stands in the Hebrew it runs: " And the *petsirah* was a *pim* for the ploughshares." The meaning of *petsirah* is doubtful; it is derived from a verbal root meaning " to push, drive, urge "; and it is the word translated (by guesswork, and with little resultant sense) " file " in the English version. *Pim* was equally obscure until recent excavations, and then the word was completely explained. Small weights of stone and of bronze have been found with this word cut upon them, evidently the name of a standard unit. One such weight, found at Gezer, was nearly 112 grains in weight. This is approximately three times a weight found long before at Samaria, called on its inscription " quarter *netseph*," and weighing close on 40 grains. A number of weights have been found marked " *netseph*," that is, " half "—presumably meaning " half shekel." These weights make the passage clear. We may translate " The setting of the ploughshares " (or, perhaps, " The fee extorted for [setting] the ploughshares ") " was three-eighths of a shekel."

The Greek version then goes on to read, " And the tools were three shekels per tooth, and for the axe and for the scythe the setting was the same." The Hebrew is in sad confusion: as it stands it reads, " And for the *ets* " (we do not know exactly what manner of tool an *et* may have been) " and for three [she]kel[s] . . . and for the axes and for fixing of the goad." We can now see that the Greek text is probably right in reading " three shekels," though perhaps " a third of a shekel " was the original version. Three letters follow, not to be translated as they stand, but doubtless the source of the Greek translators' " tooth." Making use of the two versions, we may translate the passage freely in some such way as this : " And the harvest was ready for reaping ; and the Philistines charged three-eighths of a shekel to sharpen the ploughshares ; and for the *ets* three shekels per edge, and the same for the axes and for mounting the ox-goads." The point no doubt is that these charges were ruinously exorbitant ; the Philistines took every advantage of the monopoly which they so jealously safeguarded. The verse is not yet absolutely free from difficulty, for we have not yet found out the exact shade of meaning of *petsirah ;* but we now know the lines on which it is to be interpreted, thanks to the inscribed weights which recent excavations have yielded.

Ramessu III is the last Egyptian king who leaves his name in the great fortress of Beth-Shean. He was, indeed, the last really great king of Egypt. His overwhelming defeat, in the earliest sea-fight on record, of the allied tribes called " Peoples of the Sea," who had sought to make themselves masters of the wealth of Egypt, had momentous consequences for Palestine ; for the defeated invaders, driven back from Egypt, settled upon its sea-coast, and became the Philistines, who play so important a part in the early history of the country. Ramessu was unable, or did not care, to prevent this colonisation. But the Philistines grew rapidly in strength so soon as they had established themselves; before long they had made themselves the most powerful element in the population of the country of their adoption.

The feeble kings who followed Ramessu III were unable to keep even his nominal hold over Palestine. The embassy of Wen-Amon, about a hundred years after Ramessu III, is an ample proof of this. He was sent to purchase timber from Lebanon, for the purpose of building a sacred barge for the sun-god. The goal of his voyage was Byblos, then dominated by the people called Zakkala, who were certainly another group of the "Peoples of the Sea" and closely related to the Philistines. He stopped on the way at the Zakkala town of Dor, the modern Tantura, whose king received him hospitably; but when a sailor from his ship absconded with the money with which Wen-Amon had been entrusted for the purchase of the timber, the king was not sufficiently interested to follow up the thief. Wen-Amon therefore sought to recoup himself by stealing the money of some one else, and then he made his way to Byblos, the king of which town ordered him to begone. Had not one of the king's pages been seized with a fit of mantic hysteria, in which he called upon the king of Byblos to admit the messenger of the Egyptian god,

Wen-Amon would never have been received at the court. As it was, he was summoned, but treated with very scant courtesy. The king produced his accounts, and showed him the prices that had previously been paid for timber; and obliged him to send to Egypt for further remittances. He informed him that a previous king of Egypt had sent him envoys whom he had kept in durance for fifteen years; and that their graves were to be seen hard by. At last the timber was delivered on the shore; but then Wen-Amon had to face the owners of the money which he had stolen at Dor. He managed to escape, but was driven by contrary winds to Cyprus, where the loss of the concluding portion of the papyrus compels us to leave him. In the above abstract we have not done justice to the graphic narrative, written by Wen-Amon himself, and to the clear evidence which it affords of the contempt into which Egypt had fallen at the time.

The fortress of Beth-Shean passed from Egyptian to Philistine control. Undoubtedly it was the military base from which their armies sallied forth to their victorious fight at Gilboa; and to its walls, as we can hardly doubt, the triumphant host affixed the body of their slaughtered enemy. The excavation of Beth-Shean has shown that the Egyptian fortress stood until just about the time of David, when it was destroyed by fire. This would exactly fit in with the literary indications. The valiant men of Jabesh-Gilead performed no small feat when they rescued the body of their erstwhile benefactor from its degradation. It was not merely an act of military boldness to enter a hostile city and to steal from its fortress wall a treasured trophy: it meant a tremendous fight with superstitious terrors as well. For the fortress of the uncircumcised Philistines was necessarily an unclean place. A dead body was *ipso facto* unclean, but one which had hung in a Philistine fortress would have had a double measure of taboo. That was why they considered it necessary, in violation of all Semitic instincts, to *burn* the body when they had become possessed of it. This act is alone sufficient to indicate what they risked, or thought they risked, in their adventure.

We have no actual account of a Davidic attack upon Beth-Shean, but he can hardly fail to have assaulted this important fortress in the course of his operations against the Philistines. We may confidently join with its excavators in assigning to David its final destruction.

But here we are anticipating. As yet David is a very minor personality; a vassal of the Philistines, reigning over a couple of tribes in Hebron. Not until the assassination of Ish-Baal did he get his chance. He united the northern tribes to his southern kingdom; but he saw at once that the administration of his new territory would be impossible unless his seat were more centralised. Between the two halves of his kingdom frowned the unconquered fortress of Jerusalem; he must make himself master there, if he was to consolidate his kingdom, and to strengthen himself for the inevitable struggle with the Philistines for supremacy.

The capture of Jerusalem was no trifling undertaking, as the reader who has perused the previous chapter will understand. The fortress was guarded by immense walls perched on the summit of lofty precipices. There was but one accessible side, on the north; and the only source of water was immediately under the walls, and could be defended by bowmen from the walls. It is not surprising that the Jebusites boasted of their impregnability, and shouted from the top of the hundred-feet high precipices, that towered above David's head, contemptuous taunts of their puny adversary.

But let us turn to the passage which describes David's operations. Like the passage which we have just discussed, it has long been recognised as being of especial difficulty. In parts it is corrupt to unintelligibility; and certain explanatory glosses, that were at some time written in the margin of a copy, and have become incorporated with the text, complicate rather than elucidate the difficulties. This can best be shown by a literal rendering, in which the glosses are printed by themselves:

" And the king and his men went to Jerusalem against the Jebusites, who dwelt in the land. And he [that is, 'The Jebusite'; singular for collective, in accordance with Hebrew idiom] spake to David, saying: Thou shalt not come in hither, but the blind and the lame will drive thee away.

(Meaning, David cannot come in hither. But David took the citadel of Zion, which is 'David's Fort'.)

" And David said on that day: Every one that smites

a Jebusite. And let him ascend by the *tsinnor*. And the lame and the blind. They hated. The soul of David.

(Wherefore they say: A blind and a lame man shall not enter the House.)

"And David dwelt in the Citadel and called it 'David's Fort.'"

The two passages printed in smaller type are evidently glosses. The first is an explanation of the taunt of the Jebusites, and a comment on its futility. The second is an attempt to explain a point of law, which in fact has nothing to do with the incident. The removal of these intrusions is the first necessary step towards making sense of this difficult passage. (In reading in the first of the above verses "the blind and the lame shall drive thee away" we follow a probable emendation by Wellhausen.)

The attempts that have been made to extract sense from the verse that lies between the two glosses are many and various. It is quite obvious that the text is in confusion, and, as it stands, is incoherent. One interpretation makes the verse say that David prohibited his followers, on pain of death, from inflicting any slaughter upon the Jebusites, and "on the blind and the lame, whom David's soul hateth *not*." Such a clement proclamation is, however, the last thing that we should expect from David, who whatever his other merits may have been, was ruthless in war. Another would have us to understand that the attacking party "cast the blind and the lame into the moat"; but it does not explain what part of the fortifications is intended by this word. A third explanation is to the effect that David gave orders to make all the Jebusites in the city blind and lame, by " smiting their joints." The Greek translators, who seem to have been faced with a text not essentially different from ours, rendered it more or less conjecturally thus : " Let every one that smiteth a Jebusite, assault with a dagger the blind and the lame, and those that hate the soul of David."

All these renderings depend on the sense to be given to the word *tsinnor*. This is a very rare word, used in late Hebrew in the sense of " pipe " or " conduit." It occurs only once elsewhere in the Old Testament : in Psalm xlii 7, where it is translated " waterspouts."

Unfortunately the word has disappeared from the parallel version of the story contained in I Chronicles xi. With the *tsinnor*, " the blind and the lame " have likewise dropped from the pages of the Chronicler. But this version adds a very important detail to the narrative. It tells us simply that the Jebusites said to David, " Thou shalt not come in hither." Thereupon David issued the proclamation that, " Whosoever first smiteth the Jebusites, he shall be chief and captain." The energetic Joab won the prize, and from thenceforth his life, for good or for evil, was linked with the life of his master.

Combining the two narratives, we may make out something of the order of events. David came to the city. Above him towered the great precipices, which were doubtless higher and steeper than they are now. On the summit of the precipices rose the great wall, 20 feet thick.

How high it may have been we have no idea, but even yet, after thousands of years of neglect and depredation, over twenty feet are still standing. Up to the top of the wall came the Jebusites, and flung their jeers at the invader. We may presume that the greater part of David's camp would be established near the Virgin's Fountain, for the sake of access to the water, even although it was exposed to assault from missiles.

"Dost *thou* indeed seek to enter this city? The very blind and cripples would suffice to keep thee out!" Such was the substance of the taunt, by which David was bitterly stung. He turned it back on its authors. "Smite those blind and lame ones, whom David's soul hateth!" is most probably the sense which he wished to convey, although it has been so grievously obscured by a copyist. The Jebusites had referred to those who were afflicted among themselves; David applies the epithets to the whole garrison. To suppose, as some commentators seem to have supposed, that the Jebusites actually committed the charge of their walls to blind and cripples, as a practical expression of their contempt of David, is surely to display a singular lack of any sense of humour!

"Smite those blind and lame ones! Go up the *tsinnor* and do so! and he that doeth it, will I make my general!" This was the content of David's proclamation. When we set it forth thus, we have little difficulty in identifying the *tsinnor*. The city walls were to all appearance impregnable, the city gates fully defended. David might batter at them for

TOWERS OF THE JEBUSITE CITY WALL, JERUSALEM.

It was probably from the top of the bastion in the foreground, which overhangs the Virgin's Fountain, that the Jebusites shouted their taunts to David.

months without making any impression. But there was a little postern gate into the city which it might never occur to the Jebusites to defend, for it would seem almost impracticable. This was the water-shaft, whereby they had provided for themselves access to the water of the spring; the shaft discovered in the excavation of Warren, and now known by his name.

David knew of this secret entry to the city. Perhaps it was no secret; it is difficult to keep a secret in the East, if it is worth anyone's while to divulge it. Elisha needed no supernatural clairvoyance to be able to tell to the king of Israel what secrets the king of Syria uttered in his bedchamber. Quite likely there were traitors in the Jebusite fortress who for some private grievance were ready to tell David of the city's weak spot; but equally likely the elaborate installation of which David's followers were now to make use was well known over the whole land of Canaan. Joab and his chosen men, under cover of the darkness of night, entered the cave and descended the steps. I myself followed his example when I explored the tunnel; I passed through at dead of night, without any of the villagers knowing anything about it, so as to avoid any awkward *contretemps* such as is alluded to on p. 121, *ante*. Wading through the water in the cave, carrying their weapons and, probably, a rope, they entered the tunnel that opens in the back of the cave. They would follow it westward for about 32 feet, after which it turns abruptly northward, and runs for some 23 feet, by a branch passage impassable except at oracles are dumb. Letters cannot have been unfamiliar to a people who produced a literature of such supreme magnificence. A historical sense cannot have been lacking in the people who first of all nations produced a national history. There *must* have been a rich harvest of monumental inscriptions at one time. And if this be so, they must all have perished by violence, in the way which we have already set forth. If, as seems since recent excavation to have been the case, Simon Maccabaeus planed off the city of the Hebrew kings from the Eastern Hill, and cast it, *tohu-bohu*, into the Tyropoeon Valley, on account of a passing military necessity, he would have had scant courtesy for an inscription that happened to mention a divine name which he considered heathenish.

This loss of all ancient Hebrew inscriptions is the more regrettable, because the existing record of the Hebrew monarchy is not really a history, nor is it intended as such. It is a religious essay ; a homily on the events of the monarchy in their relation to the Divine, a study of the ways of a God of purity in dealing with sinful man. The history is a mere framework ; the author selects his incidents with reference to the end which he has in view, and to no other. He neither attempts nor does he accomplish a strictly political history. If no Hebrew literature had survived, and if we were dependent for our knowledge of Hebrew history upon the testimonies of Moabite or of Mesopotamian, the king who would stand out in boldest relief would be Omri. In the Book of the Kings he is swept aside with a contemptuous sentence or two. And yet he was the oppressor of Moab; he founded the one and only city which the Hebrews added to the map of the country of which they had taken possession; he built therein a great palace, of which we can now see the foundations; in far-off Assyria his kingdom was known till long after his death, as the "Land of Omri." Even Jehu, who destroyed his dynasty half a century after his time, is supposed by the Assyrian chroniclers to have been a "son of Omri." On the other hand, Ahab, who figures prominently in the Biblical record as a foil for the religious hero Elijah, makes but little impression upon contemporary history. He had a share in the great battle of Karkar, where the Assyrians defeated a coalition headed by the king of Syria; but the writer of the Book of Kings completely ignores this important event.

It must therefore be confessed that the harvest of material, illustrative of the political history of the Hebrew monarchy, which excavation in the land of Palestine has yielded, is most disappointingly small. Here and there we may find traces of breaches and of repairs to city walls. In most cases these are undoubtedly the marks of military operations, although we may occasionally permit ourselves to admit the possibility of earthquakes being the effective cause. Palestine is a land of earthquakes. The frightful calamity which destroyed the town of Safed in 1837 is even yet vividly remembered there. A prodigious earthquake must have taken place in the days of Uzziah. It made a deep impression

treated rather as a source of irrigation than of drinking-water. At present the water is unpleasantly brackish to the taste; but we are not entitled to assume that this was always the case, for some contamination may have come in contact with the hidden source of these waters in more recent times. But if the water was always thus impregnated with salt, there is little wonder that the people of the city would prefer to drink the fresh rain water that they stored in their cisterns. At present the more prominent people of Silwan prefer to fetch their drinking-water from the great reservoir in the Haram enclosure, rather than to draw the spring water from the cave. The spring is at their very doors, and the Haram is at the end of a steep and toilsome climb; but as they pack off their womenkind to perform the service, this inconvenience is a trifle of no importance.

Here, then, there was an inexhaustible supply of water running down the valley, fertilising vegetables of which the Assyrian host would make use, and offering richly to the Assyrian army the first of all necessities. No competent leader could possibly allow such a state of affairs to continue. Hezekiah, therefore, put the Old Pool of Siloam out of action; constructed another pool, just inside the city wall; and starting from the bend in the old Jebusite tunnel, he prolonged it to the total length of 1758 feet, connecting the spring with his new reservoir. All the water of the spring was thus conveyed inside the city, and all the old extra-mural conduits were superseded and dried up.

Here the present author is, in private duty, bound to publish a *palinodia*. In a little book issued some years ago, entitled *A History of Civilisation in Palestine*, he recollects speaking rather disdainfully of the Siloam Tunnel. At the time he had not been more than a few yards into it at each end ; and he had read the descriptions of the painful experiences of Warren and others who had explored it. But sufficient allowance was not made for the fact that in those days the tunnel was silted up with about two thousand years' accumulation of mud. It has since then been completely cleared, and the author has had an opportunity of traversing it from end to end. Now that it is possible to see the whole work unencumbered, it is clearly a much more notable achievement than anyone in former days could have suspected. Where Warren was crouched between floor and roof, taking observations with a prismatic compass as the water rose above his ears, the visitor now walks upright, with the roof four or five feet, or more, above his head. The flow of the water is much more continuous now than it was when the tunnel was so much choked up ; its depth naturally varies with the rise and fall of the intermittent spring. When the writer went through, the water was waist-deep.

Notwithstanding this improved view of the undertaking, the defective engineering skill, which made the tunnel so tortuous that it must be nearly twice as long as it need have been, is not to be explained away. We know from the famous inscription, which happily escaped the

Of this Assyrian period we have a few interesting relics. First come two cuneiform tablets found at Gezer; unfortunately fragmentary, but sufficient remains to show the nature of the documents. They are both contracts, relating to the sale of property.

The first is dated on the 17th day of the month Sivan, 649 B.C. This date is expressed by naming the eponymous officer after whom the *previous* year had been called; for the folk of Gezer had not yet received news of the name of the eponym for the current year. Sivan was the third month of the year; the date mentioned would be about the end of May. Two Assyrians, by name Marduk-eriba and Abi-eriba, covenant together with regard to the sale of a house belonging to one Luakhe, including in the estate a slave by name Turiaa, his two wives, and his son. The rest of the inventory is lost. We do not learn by what right these people thus deal with Luakhe's property. A guarantee is given that the slaves named are free from physical disabilities, the nature of which is not quite certain: and the document ends with the names of twelve persons who are witnesses to the transaction. There are four Assyrians; then comes the governor of the city, whose name shows him to have been an Egyptian—it is notable that notwithstanding his official position he has had to wait until the supercilious Assyrians have had their names entered by the clerk. After the governor comes the signature of a Levantine middleman, who probably negotiated the affair; and then come five more Assyrians.

TABLET RELATING TO THE SALE OF NETHANIAH'S LAND, FOUND AT GEZER.

One of these Assyrian witnesses bore the name Zerukin. This person was called upon a couple of years later to act once more in a similar capacity. The second tablet, which recorded this fact, referred to the sale of the land of a certain Hebrew, by name Nethaniah. Nethaniah's land abutted on the property of one Sini, but we have no means of knowing where it was, though no doubt it was somewhere in the neighbourhood of Gezer. Here again the tablet is broken, and the details of the transaction are lost to us. The names of three witnesses, including Zerukin, are preserved, as well as the date—4th of Shebat is the eponymy of Akhi-Ilai, viceory of Carchemish. Akhi-Ilai's eponymy was known to be 697–8 B.C., but until this tablet was discovered it was not known that he was viceroy of Carchemish. Shebat was the eleventh month of the year ; a day in the latter half of January is indicated.

Another monument of the Assyrian domination may be seen in some curious fragments found at Tell es-Safi. They formed part of a tablet of stone bearing a carving in relief ; but it was impossible to fit them together. Conspicuous was a bearded head, with an Assyrian cast of countenance, and a device which has been explained by Albright as an endeavour to represent a ship run upon rollers. Albright refers to an incident in Assyrian annals which he supposes to be represented by this figure, and upon it he bases his adherence to the identification of Tell es-Safi with Libnah rather than with Gath.

But meanwhile the Southern Kingdom was tottering to her fall. Jerusalem was sacked in 586 B.C. The Temple was destroyed ; Zedekiah, the last king of the Hebrews, was carried off into captivity ; and the walls were broken down. After a season Persian succeeded to Babylonian, and presently certain leaders of the Jewish people found favour in the sight of their new lords. Nehemiah returned to rebuild the walls. Ezra returned to build the people's religious faith. Zerubbabel returned for the more delicate purpose of restoring the monarchy, and it is not very difficult to make a probable conjecture as to what became of him in consequence, though the historians have agreed to veil his fate in silence. There can be little doubt that some parts of the walls found by Bliss were fragments of the work of Nehemiah : but the work of Ezra was hardly such that it could leave tangible monuments. The poor little Second Temple, of which Haggai could not choose but speak disdainfully, must have been entirely cleared away to make room for the Temple of Herod.

It is to somewhere about this time that the " royal stamps " on the jar-handles are ascribed. I have on previous occasions called attention to some remarkable coincidences between the inscriptions upon these stamps, and a genealogical fragment described as an " ancient record," preserved at the end of I Chronicles iv, and ending, " These were the potters . . . (who) dwelt with the king for his work." When I find vessels stamped with the inscription, " For the king," followed by one or other of the names

Hebron, Soco, Ziph, Mimshat: when I find a record such as that just referred to, containing such names as "Ziph son of Jehallelel," "Heber the father of Soco," "Laadah the father of Mareshah"—remembering that *Heber* differs from *Hebron*, in Hebrew spelling, only by the loss of a single letter, and *Mareshah* differs from *Mimshat* (however this latter name is to be vocalised) only by two letters; remembering also that it is in proper names, and in numbers, that scribal errors most frequently creep into a text transmitted by a succession of penmen, —when I find these points of contact, I cannot regard them as mere coincidences. Certain deductions that I offered, starting from this observation, were severely criticised by Prof. Driver in his *Schweich Lectures*, and I do not venture to repeat them here. But I still hold that there cannot but be some sort of connexion between the stamps and the "ancient record" incorporated in Chronicles. We have still to determine who or what the "king" referred to may have been, and how these potters could be said to "dwell with him" if he was really a distant Persian potentate, or even a mere abstraction whose name certified that the jars bearing the marks conformed to a fixed royal standard of capacity. Both of these theories have been put forward. But more light is needed, both on the jar-handles and on the passage in Chronicles.

These are not the only enigmatical inscriptions on jar-handles that excavation in Palestine has yielded. There is another group inscribed with the letters YH. This was by some regarded as being the initials of, or an abbreviation for, the sacred name written in the vowelless Hebrew script YHWH (Yahweh, " Jehovah "). Intrinsically this is very improbable, and it has been finally disproved by other handles giving the word in full. It is a word of four letters, but quite unintelligible.

Alexander the Great delivered the ancient empire of Babylon from the yoke of the Persian conqueror. A fitting tribute to his greatness was paid by certain wealthy citizens of Sidon, whoever they may have been, who commissioned a Hellenic sculptor of consummate ability to prepare a noble sarcophagus, which is now one of the chief treasures of the Imperial Museum of Constantinople. The panels on the side of this great work of art bear a record of the achievements of Alexander, sculptured in high relief. But on the other hand, Alexander's early death made the unhappy land of Palestine the prey of warring kingdoms, which sprang from Alexander's empire. Palestine lies between Egypt and Syria; and so Palestine became the cockpit in which Ptolemy and Seleucid fought one another for over a century.

There are few very evident traces of the shuttlecock existence which the country endured during this distracting time. The absence of permanent structures, of inscriptions, of works of art, is itself a symptom of unrest and discouragement. The high hopes with which the returned exiles came back to their ancestral homes are voiced in some of the Psalms that belong to that time of short-lived happiness. Their utter disillusionment is expressed by such pessimistic writers as the authors of Ecclesiastes and of the book called Malachi; and this disillusionment is also reflected in the lack of aspiration, to which the remains associated with this epoch of history only too clearly testify. Ptolemaic coins are common in the country. Inscriptions are rare, although part of an inscription mentioning the name of Arsinoe came to light at Tell Sandahannah. Such inscriptions as exist testify to the gradual Hellenisation of the land, which is so bitterly deplored by the author of the Book of Jubilees and other nationalistic Jewish writings. Typical of the unstable condition of the nation is the history of its most prominent family, the Maccabees. The earlier heroes of this household fought the battles of the Lord, probably, with single minds and with pure motives: but before long the lust of conquest and of temporal power began to eat into them like a canker. The relations between Judas Maccabaeus and the Syrian general Nicanor are by no means easy to understand on the assumption of a whole-hearted loyalty of Judas to the Jewish cause. His brother and successor, Jonathan, was a mere worldling, whose association with the disreputable upstart Alexander Balas was thoroughly discreditable, and whose chief interest lay in the pomp and trimmings of his trumpery little court. Simon, the last of the brethren, was stabbed by his own son-in-law while he was under the influence of a drunken debauch. As for the later representatives of

Inscriptions in tombs are almost all written in Greek; only rarely are they found in Hebrew —the one important exception is the epitaph of the Beni Hazer in the Kidron Valley. When the folk of Marissa, who were much given to superstitious practices, wrote imprecatory tablets, they wrote them in Greek, even when their names show us that they were Semites. While Christ's mother-tongue was doubtless Aramaic, and while He used Aramaic on occasions of especial emotion, He must have made large use of Greek both in public and in private: otherwise, why should His occasional use of what are, after all, very ordinary and commonplace Aramaic words be so carefully reported? It is not likely that Pilate could speak Aramaic; yet he had a solitary interview with Christ, apparently without any interpreter. Christ must therefore have spoken either Greek or Latin on that occasion. In that polyglot country it would be a commonplace thing even now, for a man in the humble social station which our Lord was pleased to occupy, to be able to converse in three or four languages. What is still more remarkable and suggestive, the inscription lately discovered by Capt. Weill, recording the erection of a synagogue, is written in Greek, and the writer goes so far as to Hellenise his name Jonathan, turning it into "Theodotos."

Let us pause for a moment to consider this inscription, which raises some interesting questions. It may be translated thus—

"Theodotos son of Vettenos, priest and ruler of a synagogue, son of a ruler of a synagogue, grandson of a

THE INSCRIPTION OF THEODOTOS.

ruler of a synagogue, built this synagogue for the reading of the Law and the teaching of the Precepts ; and the hospice, and the chambers, and the installations of water, for the use of those from abroad in need thereof. Which synagogue his fathers founded, and the elders, and SIMONIDES."

The name of Simonides is written in letters of extra size. The reader is supposed to know all about him ; he must have been a person of rank, influence, or wealth. But we are in the position of a stranger, passing through an unfamiliar town, and noticing on the front of a public building, " This stone was laid by——" some local worthy, whose fame has never reached his ears. There is something pathetic in the big letters in which Theodotos sets forth the name of his patron ; it is meant to come as a grand climax after the fathers and the elders. But the climax fizzles out like a damp squib ; the great man has gone hence, and his place knoweth him no more.

Theodotos, or Jonathan to give him his true name, was a son of Vettenos. This name is neither Hebrew nor Greek ; it is Latin, or rather a derivative from Latin. It is the kind of name that a slave of a man called *Vettius* would assume. Clermont-Ganneau has ingeniously suggested that the Vettius indicated was the very man of this name who acted for Cicero as his agent in money matters ; and further, that the person called, or calling himself, Vettenus, had been one of the Jews who were carried off into slavery by Pompey (63–64 B.C.). These returned to their homes not long afterwards ;

and they were the probable founders of the *Synagogue of the Freedmen*, or, as it is called in Acts vi 9, *of the Libertines*. The community so called were the chief opponents of Stephen the protomartyr, as we learn from the passage cited. It may well be that the synagogue which Theodotos built was this very synagogue. People who had themselves suffered the misery of being strangers in a strange land might well have been moved to establish a well-equipped hostel for the reception of their co-religionists, coming from abroad. If the identification be sound, Theodotos might have been at work on his building at the time when the boy Jesus visited the Temple; and who can say that the hand that traced these letters was not among the hands that cast the stones thirty years afterwards, on the day when the seedling Church was first watered with the blood of a martyr?

We must not pass over in silence the work of that very great and very evil man, Herod the Idumæan, who took up the authority that was dropped from the nerveless hands of the last of the Maccabaeans. Herod was an ambitious man. He found himself on the throne of Solomon; and he set himself to emulate the traditional glory of that king of old. He would beautify his capital with all manner of costly buildings. He threw his whole power and influence into the Hellenising scale; buildings of a kind appeared in Jerusalem such as had never before been seen there—a Gymnasium, where, to the scandal of those who opposed these innovations, nude youths took part in the games

A CORNER OF "ABSALOM'S PILLAR."

Note the false classicism: an *Ionic* colonnade surmounted by a *Doric* frieze and an *Egyptian* cornice.

as in Greece ; a Theatre, at which, we can hardly doubt, the gross and worthless dramas of the Classical decadence were performed. It is impossible to withhold sympathy from the stern Chasidim, the purity party of ancient Judaism, who resisted these innovations as well as they could ; for all that the Chasidim were simply the earlier generation of Pharisees, and the Pharisees have a bad name in Christendom. I myself could realise something of their feelings in revisiting Jerusalem after a long absence. The veneer of a fourth-rate Europeanism which recent political changes have made possible, is as odious to one who knew the city in former days as the veneer of a fourth-rate Hellenism must have been to one of the Chasidim. I could understand the sentiments of a Chasid, perusing a programme of a performance in Herod's Theatre, when I saw a poster advertising a cinema, which offered the following hectic attractions :

MADNESS
a very beautiful tragedy
WAR AND DEATH
a very impressionable (*sic*) drama

But Herod's Gymnasium and his Theatre are still undiscovered. The foundations of much of his work, however, still remain in the city ; the substructures of his great Temple and the towers of his Palace are conspicuous. When the Pro-Jerusalem Society has finished its noble task of removing the Turkish accumulations from the interior of the citadel, we may hope to discover at least the foundations of the rest of the building. The Jews' Wailing Wall, where rites that are singularly reminiscent of the wailings for Tammuz, reported by Ezekiel as having been carried on inside the Temple, are still to be seen; parts of the Castle of Antonia, north of the Haram area; certain of the Aqueducts that convey water to the city; the great Reservoirs called "Solomon's Pools" as well as the chief water-stores in and around the city (Hezekiah's Pool, the Mamilla Pool, and several others)—these are all his work.

Not alone was Jerusalem thus beautified. Samaria received a Street of Columns, a Hippodrome, and a Palace. The Street of Columns has long been the most conspicuous monument of the ancient city; the other remains were exposed, or at least fully worked out, in the recent excavations. At Jerusalem there was also a Street of Columns, which ran axially through the city from north to south, and which is one of the most conspicuous details on the Madeba map. A few pillars, now embedded in the masonry of small shops, still remain. This, however, belongs to the time of Hadrian.

Ascalon, again, was enriched with imposing buildings. An elaborate Basilica with apsidal end was discovered in the excavation that took place there in the years following the war, as well as other public buildings (including a Theatre), and several very excellent pieces of statuary. Among these were a really beautiful figure of Victory, and a less excellent, but still good, figure of Tyche. In the Jerusalem Museum is a portrait bust from Ascalon which

PORTRAIT BUST FROM ASCALON.

is a notably clever piece of work, although the subject is a woman with a particularly evil and repulsive face.

There is much more work to be done in studying the still imposing remains of Herodian Palestine; Herodian buildings still await excavation. Archæology in Palestine suffers from an embarrassing mass of work to be got through, and a dearth of both men and money to accomplish it. It is only natural that the earlier periods should command the first consideration. But while we are digging the tell, the later relics are apt to be neglected; the Herodian palaces and buildings of luxury, the Byzantine churches, the Crusader churches and castles. All of these demand attention; and while we are busy here and there, they are slowly but surely crumbling away. Except the structures at Samaria and at Ascalon, most of the remains of the Herodian period have been found by accident. The inscription of Herod's Temple, found by Clermont-Ganneau—one of the greatest discoveries of a historical monument ever made in the country—was not found by excavation; it was lying loose in a small deserted cemetery. We have another epigraphic link with Herod's Temple in the ossuary of Nicanor of Alexandria, now in the British Museum, which was found in a tomb on the summit of the Mount of Olives. It bears an inscription in Greek, which signifies, "The ossuary of Nicanor of Alexandria, who made the doors," and in Hebrew, "Nikanor Aleksa." This clearly identifies the box as the reliquary of the wealthy

Jew of that name who is known to have made or presented to the Temple the " Beautiful Gate " of which we read in Acts iii 2.

The destruction of Jerusalem under Titus made a complete break in the history of the city. All traditions were snapped ; practically all the buildings were destroyed. Once more might a Psalmist have said, and with yet greater exactitude than was his who penned Psalm lxxix, that the heathen had laid Jerusalem on heaps. A few Latin and Greek inscriptions have come down to us from the time of Roman administration—milestones and the like. An inscription dedicatory to Jupiter Sarapis, from the time of Trajan, was discovered in the masonry of the so-called Zion Gate of Jerusalem during the excavations of Bliss. A carved head, identified as belonging to a statue of Hadrian, has been brought to light by Clermont-Ganneau. One of the most interesting relics of the Roman administration is a long inscription of which several fragments have been found at Beer-sheba, belonging to about the time of the Constantines or their successors, giving a list of towns and the amount of military tribute due from each. Clermont-Ganneau has shown a remarkable correspondence between this inscription and certain details in an imperial ordinance issued by Theodosius II in the year A.D. 409.

We can trace the gradual spread of Christianity in the country by means of the sites of early churches, some of which still preserve in whole or in part handsome mosaic pavements. A curious rock-cut chamber, possibly a church,

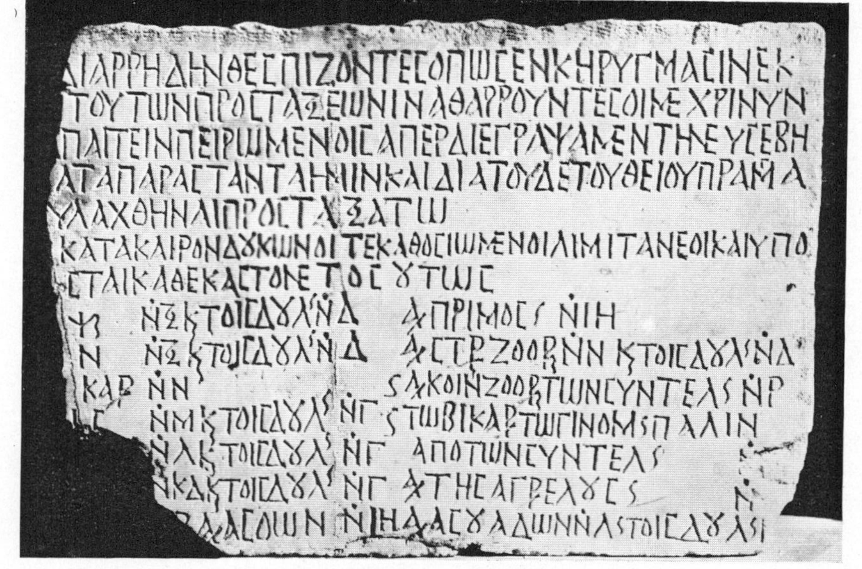

FRAGMENT OF A PROCLAMATION RELATING TO TRIBUTE, FOUND AT BEER-SHEBA.

was found by the present writer at a khirbeh called Beit Leyi, near Tell Sandahannah. A church of great antiquity was discovered by Fisher in the excavation of Beisan ; another was found by fellahin at Beit Nettif ; and others have come to light from time to time. These buildings testify to the general peacefulness of the country under the early Byzantine emperors, and to its not unsuccessful effort to cultivate Christian art. An admirable chalice, probably of the fourth or fifth century A.D., was found at or near Antioch a year or two ago as we write. Unfortunately certain preposterous claims have been made for it, presumably with the desire of enhancing its commercial value, and these have only had the effect of obscuring its real artistic merit. Such objects of ecclesiastical art, in the precious metals, are necessarily rare ; they could hardly have survived under the pressure of generations of Muslim cupidity. Probably this chalice, with some other valuable objects of metal found along with it, had been hidden in the ground, where it was discovered, at the time of the first onslaught of Islam, by some one who believed that the counsels of the false prophet must surely be brought to naught within a very few years. In the same way, the Theodotos inscription and the building-stones of the synagogue to which it had belonged, were found carefully stored in a cistern ; doubtless that they might be put together again at some more propitious season. One of the numerous caves of Tell Sandahannah contains a large number of drums of columns, probably part of some building which, in the same way, still awaits reconstruction. *Until this tyranny be overpast*, said those who made these deposits, one to the other, as they turned away from the place where they had left their precious relics; but alas! in each case the word of hope was but an epitaph. *Vanitas vanitatum, omnia vanitas.*

Of the mosaic pavements that the country has yielded, by far the most important is the great map of Palestine, dating from about the sixth century, and now preserved in the floor of a Greek church at Madeba. It was only just rescued from ignorant destruction, which wrought considerable damage to this unique monument before it was stayed. The plan of Jerusalem is especially informing: most interesting is the pictorial record which it preserves, the only one extant, of the pillar that once stood in front of the Damascus gate, and gave that structure the name which it still bears in Arabic, "Gate of the Column."

The Arab remains of Palestine—castles, houses, and mosques—can hardly be said to be available for excavation, though some of them would well repay an investigation of the kind. For the present we can do little more than study these structures as they appear above ground. Many of them are worthy of such study; they display the great artistic skill which burst forth in the early days of Islam, and the ingenuity with which the religious limitations imposed by Islam were surmounted. The use of natural forms as motives of decoration being prohibited, the artists were thrown back on conventional and geometrical forms, from which they evolved a decorative art of great beauty. The Arabic alphabet, although its practical deficiencies make it a serious obstacle to an acquisition of the Arabic language, is one of the most elegant of scripts, and it lends itself to artistic treatment; the ingenious bends into which artists and scribes distort these gracefully flowing curves can scarcely be read except by an expert, but are of an effect eminently satisfying to the eye. In contrast to this, few things are more pathetic than the occasional attempts to be seen in the streets of modern Jerusalem, to force the stiff ungainly letters of the square Hebrew script into monograms and decorative devices.

The remains of the Crusader period are castles and churches. The masonry of these buildings are easily recognised, as the dressing of the stones has a peculiar character that the masonry of no other period possesses. It consists of closely set fine lines, running diagonally across the face of the stone; very often a mason's mark, which sometimes takes the form of a European alphabetic letter, is cut over the marks of the dressing. Crusader castles are sometimes a nuisance, because they are set on the tops of mounds which cannot be dug without removing them. This, for example, is the case of the fine mound of Belameh (Ibleam). It is curious to note in passing, as an illustration of the complete subjectivity of some of the old identifications of Holy Places, that the traveller Morison was told at the end of the seventeenth century that this was the building in which Christ healed the ten leprous men.

Great results have rewarded the excavator in Palestine. Greater surprises are still, I have no doubt, in store. And yet, how small a part of the fleeting shadow that we call " life " can the excavator capture, after all! A few pages back we had occasion to refer to a certain Zerukin, who witnessed two business transactions at Gezer. Zerukin, by doing so, served a very useful purpose, not only to his contemporaries, but also to the excavator who revealed him to the modern world. For, when the first tablet came to light, it was of such an unexpected nature, that doubts were openly expressed as to its provenance. It was more than hinted that the excavator had been deceived by a workman, salting the ground with a view to *bakhshish*. A year later, when a second tablet of the same kind came to light in the same place, signed by the same man, these doubts were dispelled automatically. The excavator has, therefore, good reason to cherish friendly feelings towards Zerukin. Zerukin little dreamed, when he affixed his signature to a document on that cold January day 2600 years ago, that he had performed the one action which would spread his fame, in ages then far in the future, through regions of which he had never heard. A personality that once was loved or hated; forty years of toil or of pleasure, of mingled joys and sorrows, births and bereavements, good and evil; a human soul even now fulfilling its destiny; all these are implied in the queer groups of notches and wedges that

REMAINS OF THE CRUSADER CASTLE AT BELAMEH.

spell his name. Every scratch on an ancient stone means just such a human life ; whither have they all gone, all these ghosts, of which the excavator thus catches fitful glimpses, as he lays bare the silent streets which once they walked—a macabre chorus that dins ever in his ears the words of the mediæval epitaph :

> Quisquis eris qui transieris, sta, perlege, plora ;
> Sum quod eris, fueramque quod es ; pro me precor ora.

CHAPTER IV

EXCAVATION AND CULTURAL HISTORY

THE excavator in Palestine cannot be blamed if he feels occasional twinges of envy toward his more fortunate brethren whose lot may be cast in Egypt, in Mesopotamia, or in Crete. Not for him are the palace of a Minos, the library of an Asshurbanipal, the treasures of a Tutankhamun. He must be content to turn over, month after month, the sordid relics of a sordid people, only occasionally striking a spark of excitement from them.

Yet this is not altogether without its compensation. Minos and Tutankhamun are certainly more spectacular than are the nameless and forgotten potters and housewives to whom the Palestine excavator is privileged to give a fresh lease of life upon earth. But they are spectacular because they are wholly abnormal. Now, J. R. Green and other pioneers have taught us that History is a record of

> Not kings alone, but nations,
> Not thrones and crowns, but men—

if we may quote a doggerel parody of the National Anthem which has incomprehensibly found its way into some of our hymn-books. The commonplace things of life are the true matter of life. A humdrum existence, in office, shop, or study, is the real existence of a man : the time-table of his daily routine is his essential biography. He never gets his name into the newspapers unless he does something exceptional, and off the beaten track.

So it is that from the common things, forming the ordinary yield of a Palestinian excavation, we get a truer picture of the life and culture of the country than from the deposits made in an exceptionally rich tomb. King Solomon amused himself with apes and peacocks. His subjects were compelled to pay for them, but otherwise their lives were not affected by them. Apes and peacocks were exotics, and they had no more to do with the life and culture of the country at large than the togas and sandals affected by certain eccentric folk have to do with the general culture of England.

Like most other countries the course of whose civilisation has been studied in recent years, Palestine has been found to have passed through the three stages of civilisation, when stone, bronze, and iron were respectively the materials of which the chief weapons and ornaments were made. The occupation of the land by man began at a very early date. Stone implements, indistinguishable from those of the successive stages of the European Palæolithic Age, and presumably contemporary with them, have been found, scattered over nearly its whole area. Man was privileged to see the great

Pleistocene lake that once filled the Jordan valley, of which we may see only a shrunken remnant—that perfection of serene beauty and grandeur called the Dead Sea, which has so strangely become a type of malediction and of destruction. Chellean and Acheulean flint implements have been picked up around Ramleh, near Jaffa; the plain south of Jerusalem has yielded others, as well as examples of the later stages of the Palæolithic Age (except the Solutrean, which does not appear to be represented in the country); the valleys of Galilee and of the Lebanon have also been productive of remains of this kind. No human bones have been found, except some scanty fragments from the cave of Antelias near Beirut.*

But, the Palæolithic Age is a field apart. Continuous occupation begins with the Neolithic period: excavation has carried the record of civilisation from that time onward to the time of the Arabs and the Crusaders.

It is no exaggeration to say that throughout these long centuries the native inhabitants of Palestine do not appear to have made a single contribution of any kind whatsoever to material civilisation. It was perhaps the most unprogressive country on the face of the earth. Its entire culture was derivative. Babylon, Egypt, Crete, Rome, each in its turn, lends it a helping hand; never is it stimulated to make an effort for itself. As we walk through a dirty, ill-smelling modern village, with its flat-topped

* The discovery of a Mousterian skeleton in Galilee is announced as these sheets are passing through the press.

huts of rough stone and mud, we may fancy ourselves, without any illegitimate straining of the imagination, in one of the "cities" of the rascally "kings" of the Tell el-Amarna period, or in a village of the time of Solomon, or of Ezra, or of the Gospels. Doubtless there have been changes, especially in these latter years. In villages near the larger towns, the wealthier sheikhs are indulging in incongruous luxuries, such as watches and even gramophones. But the essential background, with its ineradicable squalor, remains as it ever was.

The general impression which a modern Palestinian village makes upon the casual wayfarer is one of abject poverty. Dirty houses, populated with all manner of unpleasant insects; lean and hungry dogs; hard-faced men and women, the latter, especially, aged long before their time; tattered, almost naked children—such are the sights that rouse the pity of the passing stranger. Yet, although there is no doubt a low standard of living, we should be surprised at the result of an inquisitorial investigation of the private affairs of some of these seeming paupers. A number of years ago I was brought into contact with one of these rustic sheikhs. His house was no more attractive, hygienically, than the others in his filthy village; yet he was commonly reported to be worth several thousand pounds. He had his money in the bank. For all I know, he may have held stocks and shares in various concerns; he certainly held the title-deeds of no inconsiderable landed property; and I was told that on a certain occasion when he came within the grasp of the law, and was fined fifty pounds, he paid over the money there and then, with a contemptuous shrug of the shoulders and a grandiose manner which implied that fifty pounds was nothing to *him!*

Now if that man had lived in the days of Tahutmes III, when there were no banks or investments where he could put his money away out of reach of the spoiler, he would have been obliged to bury it in the floor of his hut. Tahutmes would have smelt it out, dug it up, and carried it off. A modern instance like that just cited makes us understand what otherwise looks quite inexplicable—how Egyptian kings could sack these miserable Palestinian towns, and carry off such an extraordinary amount of loot as that very Tahutmes claims to have carried away from the town of Megiddo.

Very rarely indeed has anything in the nature of treasure survived for the excavator to find. Two gold ingots, together worth intrinsically about £200, found in Gezer, are still practically unique. From time to time buried treasure has been found—pots of coins and the like—giving the countryfolk the mischievous idea that vast wealth is lying in the ruins, which they might secure if only they knew the magic spells that would reveal its exact hiding-place. It is alleged that at a place called Saris, a little distance west of Jerusalem, there was once an inscription in a certain cave; there certainly were two remarkable carved figures in relief, one of which still survives, or survived when I saw it many years ago. A countryman entered the cave and saw the inscription, which he supposed to be an indication of the place where the treasure was buried. He could not read it, but he dug up the earth covering the floor of the cave without finding anything: clear traces of his proceedings remained when I visited the cave. Thereafter he utterly destroyed the inscription, saying that if he could not find the treasure, at any rate no one else should. What the inscription may have been, and even in what language it may have been, is quite unknown.

Nothing will dislodge from the heads of the people the notion that excavators are merely treasure-hunters like themselves. Some even imagine, or profess to imagine, that the seemingly valueless potsherds which the digger gathers with such inexplicable care are really gold, temporarily transmuted to throw the onlooker off the scent.

But when treasure was buried in antiquity, it was in most cases never really lost to sight. If the owner died without making use of it, his heirs knew where it was and dug it up. They bartered it, dispersed it, melted it, when necessity compelled them to do so. In other cases the raider or the tax-gatherer laid hands on it; it passed, more than probably, into the possession of the king, and was finally sent to Egypt or to Assyria, as part of the blackmail paid to buy off a threatened invasion. In the rare cases when its original owners forgot it, or failed to recover it, the ultimate discovery has usually been made, accidentally, by some fortunate peasant, digging in his field for quite different purposes.

When I was conducting excavations in the country, I sometimes received letters from people offering to point out to me places where they knew gold to be buried, and bargaining to reward me, on a more or less equitable basis of division, if I put the resources of the Palestine Exploration Fund at their disposal to dig it up. Possibly it may interest and amuse the reader to see one of these curious documents, transcribed *verbatim et literatim* save for the omission of a sentence or two in which certain persons are mentioned by name. The punctuation is as in the original communication:

The cause of writing my letter is that of an early act that has been done by our relations ; My uncles' mother [he means his mother's uncle : a syntactic difference between Arabic and English has misled him] was a maconer digging the new foundation for a building to the Jews about nine or eight meters deep. As he was digging he found a great wonderfull dish with four handels covered & filled with real gold of St. Constantin and Helene. He hid five pieces & made up his mind to come at the same night with his father & his friends & open it. He covered it with some earth & stones & shouted " It is enough so deep we have found a rock. His father used at that time to come daily from Bethlehem & bring him his food. when coming at that hour showed him the place. Unfortunately to his success all maconers were collected at the night to go to Acca by the order of Abraham Pacha.

Time came & time Past till at last it was heard by the owners of the building. The owners asked about the real founder & sent after him to Acca, but to their success they received the echo " He is dead. After great trouble they asked about his father if he reminds yet the place. At that days my Grandfather & Grandmother were at Jaffa in our home : so they were taken to Jerusalem with my father & aunt riding on donkeys because they were no carriages at that time. My Grandfather, was old & was all the time shooking his head. when reaching they stayed three days of rest eating & drinking, sleeping to the expenses of the owners of the building. At last he showed them the place & told them to dig from outside ; but they dug from insid because they were afraid of the government & the rode was not wide enough. The building was left with a fee for three years, that it means no body habited it for three years. After digging & filling all the rooms they found the great stones of Prophet Solomon, at that point they stoped digging & left it alone & none heard & new about except *we* & *they* :

So once I was speaking to my father about exavicating in Jerusalem & that Dr. Frederick Bliss has found an old church under Jerusalem & a quarrel has been held between Mohamedans & Christians to whom it should be & at end it was shut up & so by talking he told me to write and ask Dr. Bliss about the story. So I wrote & wrote till at last a friend of mine told me that you has taken his place. However I dare to write you wich is sure & real act & not simply by words—You may ask about it & you will hear if it is not true or not.

A friend of mine of the Mohamedans were in talk of digging such things as his home ; because also they found hear at Jaffa a great hugeous stone of only one foot thick & more than 40 feet long. they could not find out what it is so they left it alone. At last I told him if he can help me to my story. He promised me by word of honor only if it is true act to bring me a paper by the writing of the Governor & many signs with a stamps on, that I will take a part & no difficulties & pain will be made to me but simply show them the place—I left him and did not return back to him any more.

I was a student in [an institution which he names] for three years & at last chance opposed me to come & work with misery.

If you have courage to know & dig the place write me please by the earliest opportunity that my father may go up to Jerusalem to show you & tell you from his own words. My father is seventy one years old. But dear sir you have to pay the expenses & none else—If you will digging partly with the government & we, then we will pay you twice the expense and I also will tell you about many places which will make England reach for many years. This is what I have to say ending my words. Offering you my heart, Yours sincerely, etc. etc.

After reading the long-drawn-out whine for gold contributed by King Tushratta to the Tell el-Amarna correspondence, and then perusing a letter like that which has been laid before the reader, the second half of the *Gloria Patri* irresistibly breaks away from its solemn context and enters the mind as the only possible comment : *As it was in the beginning, is now, and ever shall be, world without end !*

We may now give a synopsis of what excavation has revealed as to the material culture of the people of Palestine at different stages of their history. It will be convenient to divide the subject into a number of separate headings.

Dwellings

Some even of the modern inhabitants of Palestine dwell in caves, either temporarily or permanently ; and the wandering Bedawi knows no dwelling but his tent. As it is now, so has it been from time immemorial. The tent-dwellers are known to us from literature of the Patriarchal period as well as from the literature of modern travel. Excavation in the floor of caves reveals the evidences of ancient occupation scarcely more primitive than the relics of modern cave-dwelling families. Rude pottery, rude flint knives, piles of stones—probably ammunition collected to discourage an intrusive wolf or hyaena—these are the principal objects which such an investigation yields. As a rule the cave was occupied in its natural form, though perhaps it might be slightly adapted to convenience by knocking off awkward projections of rock.

In the neighbourhood of Beit Jibrin, in the south of Palestine, there is a widespread city of artificial caves, the existence of which a wayfarer would hardly suspect. Small holes in the hillside, difficult to discover, give admission to extensive labyrinths of passages and chambers. Many of these still await their explorer, and all of them await explanation. In various centres east of the Jordan there are similar underground excavations.

In the cities, however, the inhabitants had to build them houses. The only materials for judging of the houses that remain for us are two or three feet of walls. Very rarely indeed is enough of the wall remaining to retain a window ; in almost every case it is even ruined below the level of the door-threshold, which must normally have been raised a little above the surface of the ground. This makes it very difficult to determine the mutual relation of the chambers exposed, or even to decide where one house ends and the next begins. In the modern villages most of the houses have but one storey; but the more pretentious have two, with, in addition, a flat roof which can be used as an airy place for sitting at ease. That this was the case in ancient times is indicated by such a narrative as that of Elisha and the woman of Shunem; the house of this "great woman" was clearly two-storeyed. But no remains have yet been found of an actual two-storeyed building—or, to speak more accurately, no evidence has been found that any building exposed had an upper floor. The means of access to the upper floor, when they existed, were doubtless, as in the modern houses, external staircases of wood leading up to a balcony.

As a rule the walls were built of moderately sized stones set with a mud mortar, and probably also plastered over with a coating of mud. Fine lime cement was reserved for the cisterns, which had to be made watertight. The doors were flaps of wood, rotating on horns projecting above and below from the inner edge. These horns turned in stone cups, which are very commonly found in excavations. The windows were presumably filled with an openwork lattice of wood, as in modern houses. Window-glass does not begin to appear, so far as we can tell, until Roman times.

As in the modern villages, the roofs were flat

and covered with a layer of mud. This mud, after being dried and cracked under the hot summer sun, was renewed each year just before the winter rains were expected. Stone rollers, with which the roof was flattened down after this process, exactly similar to rollers used for the same purpose in modern times, have not infrequently been found.

It is difficult to say how long a house of this kind would remain standing ; probably not very long. At Taanach the remains of a family were found, that had suddenly been crushed to death by the fall of their dwelling. A woman, wearing her amulets and ornaments, with a knife in her hand and food-vessels lying near—a mother who had been preparing the family meal—was surrounded by five children, of ages ranging from sixteen to four. Sadly futile was the little image of Ashtaroth, suspended to the wall as a luck-bringer ! Such accidents were probably not uncommon. The rate of the growth of accumulation is not uniform ; in one place at Gezer there was an accumulation of about 40 feet between the rock-stratum (*circa* 2000 B.C.) and the top stratum (*circa* 150 B.C.). This suggests a rough average growth of a foot in a little over fifty years. But in other parts of the same mound the accumulation, extending over the same length of time, was not nearly so deep.

While as a rule stone set in mud was the material of which the houses were built, brick was also used. The bricks were generally soft baked, and of rather large size. No bricks with maker's or patron's names stamped upon them, or any other device, have been found earlier than the Roman period. Large brick buildings were unearthed at Gezer, Jericho—much of the city wall there is of brick—Beth-Shean, and some other places. It is often impossible to recover a brick building, because the soft-baked bricks have disintegrated to such an extent that they are hardly distinguishable except by their reddish-colour, from the soil in which they have been embedded.

In plan the houses seem to have been similar to the houses of the modern villages. An open courtyard, with a high blind wall that offers no loophole for the prying eyes of intruders, is turned toward the street. Inside and at the back of this courtyard is the house, of two or more rooms, varying greatly in disposition. The plans are laid down with singular irregularity; and very rarely is there anything remaining to show the purpose which the room was intended to serve. Indeed, owing to the disappearance of the doorways, we are often at a loss to determine which enclosures were open courts, and which were covered rooms. Sometimes there is a raised bench of stones or clay running along one side of a chamber. This was probably a daïs for sleeping upon. (When I first set up an excavation-camp in a country region of Palestine, one of the villagers, watching the bedstead being fitted together, plaintively remarked, "I wish we had beds like that; it would raise us up above the fleas!")

For each house, or group of houses, there was

a cistern, consisting of a bottle-shaped opening in the rock, sometimes as much as 20 feet deep, lined with well-made cement. These cisterns were often found to contain many broken water-pots, which had come to grief by being knocked too roughly against something when they were lowered into the water. Sometimes skeletons were found at the bottom of the cistern, suggesting tragedy—accident, suicide, or murder. In one cistern at Gezer there was a large number of male skeletons, associated with the upper half of the body of a young woman who had been sawn asunder at the waist.

In modern villages there are rarely any buildings other than the houses. There may be a mean little domed square shrine over the tomb of some local holy man ; there may possibly be a village guest-house ; but it is not often that there is any other public structure. In the same way, buildings other than the common houses are rare in the ancient Palestinian towns. Petrie found at Tell el-Hesy the remains of a building, possibly the governor's palace, decorated with slabs upon which Hathor-heads were suggested rather than sculptured. It seemed as though these slabs were not in the place for which they were originally intended, but had been taken from some other building ; for they were turned upside down. Later, Bliss found at the same place a building, possibly a storehouse of some sort, with a well-laid out and unusually symmetrical plan. Two large complexes of rooms, perhaps palaces, were found at Gezer ; one of these was in brick. Two large fortifications came to light in the middle of Tell Mutasellim (Megiddo) ; underneath one of these were some remarkable and richly furnished tomb-chambers. But of all these structures one thing only can be said ; the quality of the building is extremely poor.

The buildings identified as the palaces of Omri and of Ahab at Samaria were naturally more elaborate and were in a superior style of masonry. We know that when Solomon began to build grandiose structures at Jerusalem, he was unable to find local workmen competent to carry out his ideas, and had to apply to his ally, the Phœnician Hiram, to supply him with artificers. Whether Omri and Ahab were reduced to the same necessity we do not know ; but it is quite likely that Ahab, in view of his marital relations with Phœnicia, likewise imported workmen from the comparatively civilised kingdom of the north. The excavation revealed that the rock had been scarped to give a foundation for the palace, which consisted of a block of building about 160 feet square, divided into groups of rooms arranged around open courts. In the time of Ahab the palace was greatly increased. An addition, measuring over 300 feet from north to south, was thrown out westward. This consisted of a large courtyard, bounded by a wall about 16½ feet thick, with a row of rooms formed in its thickness. We are reminded of the row of chambers found in a tower of Bliss's Jerusalem wall. Inside this courtyard there was a building consisting of a number of small rooms arranged north and

PART OF THE FOUNDATIONS OF AHAB'S PALACE AT SAMARIA.

south of a central hall. The complete plan of the structure could not be recovered, as it was in a very ruined condition ; some of the walls had disappeared altogether. The masonry cannot be said to have been of fine quality ; but it was distinctly superior to the miserable masonry of the common houses.

In every case the city communities protected themselves by means of a great surrounding wall, with gates and towers. This wall was of considerable thickness. Gezer had two walls, each about 16 feet in thickness ; the city of David had been surrounded by the Jebusites with a wall 20 feet across. These walls were built with greater care than the houses. The stones used in the construction of the Jerusalem walls were of great size, but were only roughly dressed to shape with the hammer. Ornamental dressing, with combing and bossing of the exposed face of the wall, seems to begin about the time of David, but is always rare down to the time of the exile. It is really not until the influence of Hellenism began that artistically dressed stones begin to be used freely. This was not for want of examples. A single well-squared stone was found at Gezer bearing upon its surface a large hieroglyphic character, which we may assume to have been part of an inscription that once covered the façade of the structure to which the stone had belonged. This might well have been a temple of an Egyptian community.

The importance of the enclosing wall to the life of the city is shown by the care with which repairs are effected, even at the expense of pulling down the enclosed houses, as a passage which we have already quoted testifies. The inhabitants were never satisfied with their ramparts. Towers and bastions were continually being added, with the purpose of making the construction yet more impregnable. Gates had to be provided, but these were as few and as small as possible so that they could be easily defended. Large numbers of bronze arrowheads discovered scattered in the ground outside the great gate of Gezer spoke of a murderous battle having taken place there for the possession of the city. In certain towns there was an inner citadel or acropolis, to which the inhabitants could retire if they were compelled to abandon the defence of their own rampart, Inside this acropolis, the houses were identical in type with those outside it.

Implements and Weapons

The implements of stone which the Palæolithic people have left behind differ in no respect from those of the corresponding stages of the European Palæolithic. If anything, the Palestinian types appear to bear a closer relationship with those of Western Europe than with those of Eastern Europe.

In recent years doubt has been thrown on the existence of a Neolithic culture in the Near East. In an important article entitled *L'industrie néolithique et le proche Orient*, published in 1913 in the journal called *Syria*, Jacques de Morgan announces his conversion to this sceptical attitude. Formerly, with the rest of the followers of Gabriel de Mortillet, one of the fathers of prehistoric research, he had believed in a Neolithic phase preceding the appearance of metal. Under the influence of this belief he had written works on the *Origins of Egypt* and on the *Early Tombs of Negadah* (1896–7). But he had found continually, during his excavations in India, Persia, Mesopotamia, Susiana, and North Africa, that stone implements of the types commonly called Neolithic were associated with metal tools. Thus, in his great excavation of Susa, where so many epoch-making discoveries were made, he uncovered the first city, with its clay rampart and its extra-mural acropolis, resting upon the native soil, at a depth of nearly 100 feet below the present surface. This very ancient settlement contained metal tools; a fact which led him to expect to find an earlier, purely Neolithic, settlement elsewhere in the neighbourhood. But comparison of the chipped flints discovered in this bottom stratum with others of known date convinced him that here he was actually in the presence of the first colonisation of Susa. Hall's investigations on the site of Eridu confirmed this conclusion; and searching further, in Chaldea, Mesopotamia, and on the eastern slope of the Anti-Lebanon, he was led irresistibly to the conclusion that a purely Neolithic period is totally absent in this region. As yet he admits some reserve for the absoluteness of this conclusion in the regions of Ararat and of Syria, where other explorers have reported Neolithic finds; but he considers that these discoveries require re-examination. For Egypt he now entirely disbelieves in a Neolithic phase. Even in European archæology, where the Neolithic period seemed to be most completely established, he expresses considerable scepticism of a pure Neolithic phase. The famous Neolithic beds under the palaces of Cnossos and of Phæstos in Crete he considers *Æneolithic* ; and of the lowest city at Hissarlik (Troy), after noting that metal objects had been there found, he slyly adds, *et la nécessité de rencontrer le néolithique était si bien ancrée dans les esprits, qu'on s'est demandé si ces objects n'auraient pas glissé des couches supérieurs au cours des fouilles.* He notes that his predecessors had already observed the absence of Neolithic implements in Cyprus, and had sought to explain this by supposing that the people were fishers, and so did not need stone weapons and implements as much as hunters would have done ; to which he adds the sensible comment that a more rational explanation would be the total absence of Neolithic people.

"We see," concludes De Morgan, "that four great civilisations developed in the East : Chaldea and Elam, Egypt, Crete, and, later, the Hittites. Without prejudging the ethnical character of these peoples, we may say that in the ocean of the barbarous world, the region where these empires are found, formed an island of 'capacity for civilisation.' In comparison with the great mass of the continents, this region was very small ; but for deciding their destinies its importance was very great. Egypt borrows many ideas from Chaldea: Crete had relations with the land of the Pharaohs; the Hittites draw their inspiration from Mesopotamia. But these borrowings were only in matters of detail; the main lines of culture were common to all. With regard to Syria, placed between these masters in civilisation, she could do no more than yield to the impulses that fell upon her from time to time, from one or other of these. Syria was taught by contact; but her geographical position, and the relief of her surface, made it impossible that she should create an independent civilisation."

Those who have persuaded themselves, and would seek to persuade others, that Egypt alone was the mother of every manifestation of culture over the whole world, from pole to pole, will find salutary reading in this last paragraph, penned as it is by an excavator of enormous experience.

But if the revolutionary conclusions which De Morgan has thus indicated prove to be justified, we shall have to revise many of our ideas with regard to the Palestinian tells. A rude hand-made pottery, associated with flint knives, has been called Neolithic. A separate population whose dead were burnt in a cave at Gezer, has also been described by this name. Further research, in the light of these observations, will show whether such a revision is necessary. But in all cases the conclusions of an explorer must be subject to revision in the light of discoveries made subsequent to his own. Knowledge grows apace, and it is given to few to reach finality.

However we are to interpret the evidence, there is evidence for the existence of a rude non-Semitic people, who chipped flint knives and scrapers, who dwelt in caves, and who burnt their dead. Certain of the caves at Gezer contained metal tools, or at least scraps of metal, which were explained at the time as due to later intrusion: it may be that this was not so, but that they belonged to the cave-dwellers from the first. "Prove *all* things, hold fast that which is good," is sound advice in other departments of study and activity as well as in theology.

In offering a necessarily brief description of the types of implements that Palestine excavation has yielded, it will be convenient to follow the order of the general classification of such objects set forth by the distinguished French prehistorian, M. Adrien de Mortillet. This can be set forth in tabular form thus:

IMPLEMENTS

Purpose	By pressure	By shock	By rubbing
cutting	knife plane shears	axe, adze hatchet chisel gouge	saw
scraping	scraper	—	rape, file
crushing and bruising	fabricator	hammer maul	pestle grindstone
piercing	awl	pick	drill

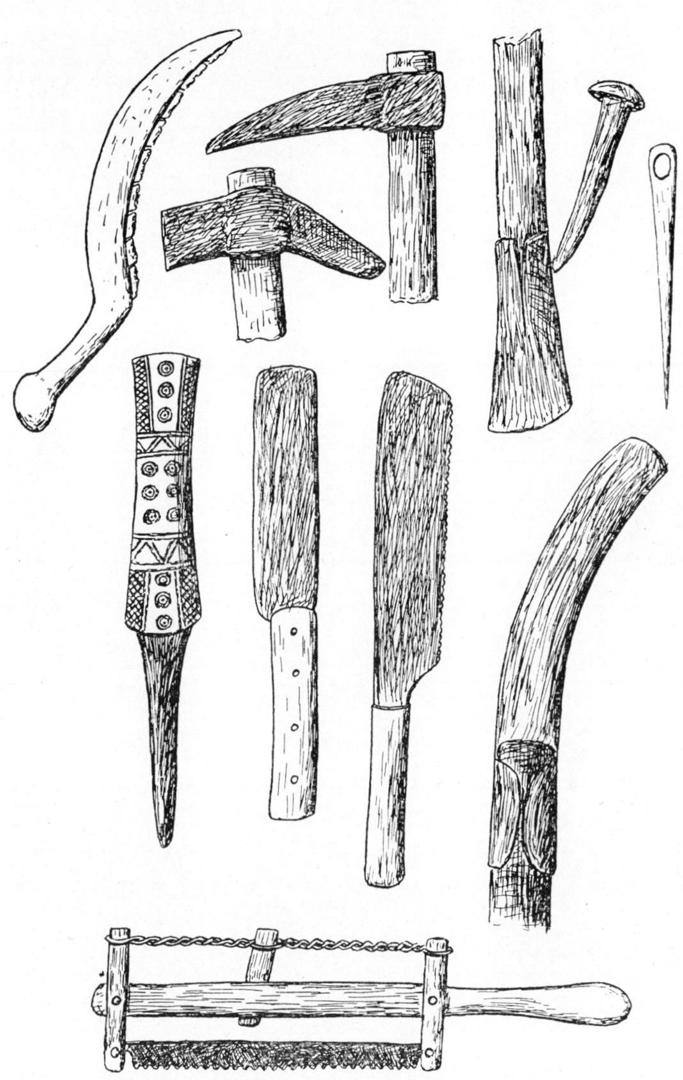

SPECIMENS OF PALESTINIAN TOOLS.

Sickle, axes, chisel, nail, needle, awl, knives, saw.

WEAPONS

Purpose	Held in hand	Mounted on shaft	Thrown
striking	coup-de-poing	club	stone blunt-headed arrow
piercing	dagger, rapier, stiletto	lance, spear	javelin harpoon arrow.
cutting	sword	hatchet halberd	boomerang chakra arrow with transverse edge

Of the tools and weapons enumerated in the above tables, many are not to be found in Palestine at all. Wooden weapons, such as clubs and boomerangs, if they were used—and we can scarcely doubt that at least the former were used, as they are by shepherds defending their flocks from wild beasts to-day—have vanished, owing to the natural decay of the material. The chakra, a weapon of certain Indian tribes, is included only for the sake of completeness ; it is unknown in Palestine, as also, apparently, is the transverse-headed arrow, although the latter appears to have been used in Egypt.

Knives were made of flint, bronze, or iron, at different stages of civilisation. The flint knives were simply " ribbon " flakes with sharp edges, sometimes a little serrated either with intention or by use. The knives of metal resembled in appearance the blades of our modern dinner-knives. They consisted of a blade with a single cutting edge and a blunt back, having a tang projecting from the butt end for fitting into a wooden or horn handle. Sometimes, however, there was no tang; instead, there were rivet-holes through the butt, by which the handle could be secured. It is to be noticed that the rivets were often of bronze, even when the blade was of iron. In most cases the handles, which were made of such perishable materials as wood or horn, have decayed away.

Nothing that could be called a plane, or a pair of shears, has come to light in Palestine excavations.

Axes of bronze resembled the flat axes of the early European bronze age. Sometimes Egyptian forms of axes, not found in Europe, come to light. The later European forms (palstaves and socketed axe-heads) are unknown. Axes and adzes of iron, resembling the modern tools, with a hole for receiving the handle, were common after the beginning of the general use of iron (say after about 1000 B.C.). A combination tool, axe and adze, with a perforation in the middle, is also found.

Chisels, tanged, in bronze, and tanged or socketed in iron, are not infrequent; but gouges are rare.

Saws are found in all three materials. They are all of small size, and consist of "ribbons" of flint, or knives of bronze or of iron, with the edges serrated. Some of the flint saws are of admirable workmanship. The metal saws were probably mounted, as in the modern East, in a stretching-frame, like the frame of a fret-saw. The large European hand-saw is rarely used in modern Palestine except by people under direct European influence; in ancient Palestine nothing like it is known.

Scrapers of flint are common: they are sometimes very handsome implements. They are wide discs, shaped like an oyster-shell, with a specially prepared edge running round the convex side. Sometimes part of the calcareous outer surface of the nodule, from which the tool was chipped, remains adhering to one side of the scraper. This occasionally bears an animal or some other device scratched upon it. We may compare the animal figures scratched upon flint implements that were found recently at "Grimes' Graves" in Suffolk, and were (not very judiciously) regarded by some as Palæolithic.

In rapes and files there is nothing to show; nor are any objects comparable with the European fabricator reported.

Hammers and mauls consist for the greater part of heavy stones, with or without a perforation for fitting them on a handle. Hammers in metal are distinctly rare.

Pestles and grindstones of stone are common. The former are of the shape which would be natural to such a tool: long cones with a slightly convex base. The latter are bowl-shaped. Flat stone bowls, supported on three feet, are also common. The stone used is always a very hard, rough stone, admirably suited by its texture to help the grinding work of the pestle. Pestles and mortars of metal are not recorded.

form important elements in the complex and mysterious caves round Beit Jibrin. They are dug up continually in the excavation of tells.

There is an immense variety of design and of size. Some of them are simply single square vats and nothing more. Others are complicated groups of vats, large and small, the exact purpose of which it is very difficult to discriminate. And it is not easy to determine in every case whether a vat was intended for crushing grapes or olives.

Without entering into minute details, which would here be inappropriate, it may be said that there were three essential elements in a fruit-press of the kind : a pressing surface, a refining-vat, and a collecting or storage vat. The fruits (grapes or olives) were spread, or placed in baskets, on the pressing surface. Grapes were pressed by treading, but olives were pressed by means of heavy weights. These were great masses of stone, in shape a truncated pyramid, with a rope-hole in the upper end. These were tied on to the end of a heavy wooden beam, the other end of which was engaged in a hole in a vertical standard. The beam thus formed a lever of the second order, the hole in the standard serving as fulcrum, the suspended weights the applied power. Under its stress the olives yielded their juice, which ran from the pressing surface into the refining-vat. Here the oil was allowed to stand until any impurities which it might contain had settled as a sediment in the bottom of the vat. When this process had been completed, a hole was opened between the vats,

A ROCK-CUT WINEPRESS.

allowing the refined oil to run into the storage-vat, and the process was begun again with a fresh supply of fruit. In some vats there remain large stone rollers with which the olives were crushed.

Turning now to the weapons, the coup-de-poing or hand-axe, a sharp-pointed oval or triangular mass of flint, is an essentially early Palæolithic contrivance, which probably served the double purpose of tool and weapon. It is not uncommon in Palestine, although it is of too early a period to find a place in the yield of a tell.

The club of the modern shepherd is a heavy bar of hard wood, about 2 feet 6 inches long. The head is a pear-shaped or egg-shaped expansion, and is studded with large flat-headed iron nails. At the other end there is a hole through which a thong can be passed, for securing the club to the hand, so that it shall not fly away through the grasp being accidentally relaxed. It weighs about 2½ pounds, and is a formidable weapon. Egg-shaped mace-heads, of a compact white stone like marble, probably of Egyptian origin, are common in the towns near the sea-coast.

Stones were, and still are, the commonest of all weapons of offence in Palestine. People throw stones at one another on very slight provocation, regardless of consequences; fortunately the aim is usually bad, as the assailant is as a rule in too violent a temper to control it. Stoning was the chief method of execution under the Mosaic law. Any and every stone in the country which a man can lift, might be regarded as a weapon.

Blunt-headed arrows are very uncommon. A cache of these tools was found in a tomb-cavern at Gezer, which yielded other interesting weapons as well. They were probably intended to kill birds that yielded ornamental plumage, which would be ruined for decorative purposes if it was dabbled with blood. Doubtless the coquettes of ancient Palestine shared the singular delusion still prevalent among their sisters in modern Europe, that they improved their appearance by attaching fragments of dead birds to various parts of their persons!

Daggers were among the commonest of weapons. They resembled knives in general appearance; but they differed in having *two* sharp edges, a wider blade, and a sharper point.

The bronze heads of lances and spears were as a rule tanged and barbed. Socketed implements and weapons in bronze are practically unknown, and in iron they are rare until the latest periods of the occupation of the tells. Javelins, meant for casting, are similar to these, but they have flat leaf-shaped blades without barbs.

Arrowheads of bronze are as a rule leaf-shaped. Barbed arrowheads are rare; in flint especially so; I myself have seen only one barbed arrowhead in flint from Palestine. Bronze arrowheads do not begin to appear in any considerable numbers until the iron age has well begun; until then, bronze, which was a material essential for all manner of imple-

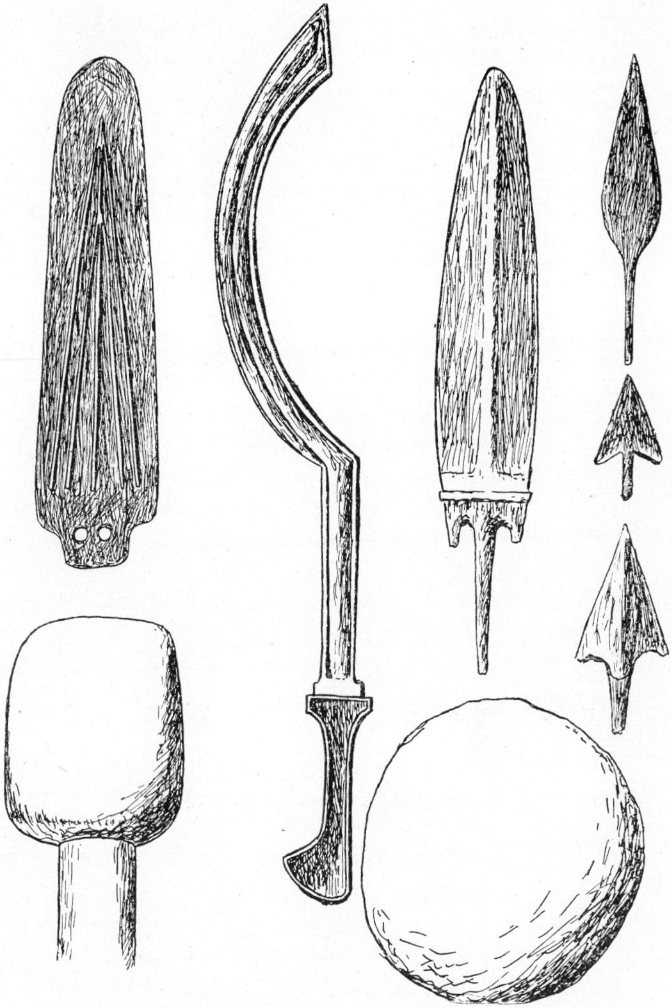

SPECIMENS OF PALESTINIAN WEAPONS.

Dagger, scimitar, sword, arrows, mace, sling-ball.

ments, was too valuable to waste on weapons which, once shot away, were fated to be lost. As there is no native tin in Palestine, the bronze must have been imported, and was therefore expensive. Iron arrowheads do not appear until close to the Roman domination. A common form of iron arrowhead, unknown in western and northern Europe, has a solid pyramidal point, with three edges, each terminating below in a barb.

Swords were short and straight-edged. The European bronze-age leaf-shaped sword is unknown. A Mycenæan sword, with horns projecting upwards from the corner of the blade, was found in the tomb-chamber that yielded the blunt-headed arrowheads already referred to. The same tomb contained a noteworthy curved scimitar of a Babylonian type.

Halberds, hatchets, as well as boomerangs and transverse-edged arrows, cannot be said to be Palestinian weapons.

Pottery

The pottery of Palestine is of capital importance for the study of the chronology of the ancient remains of the country. It is quite impossible to compress the subject of Palestinian pottery into a few pages of a book like this. In any case, the subject has scarcely more than a specialist interest, and a detailed account of it would here be hardly appropriate. We do not, therefore, attempt more than a few general words of description.

The earliest forms of pottery found in the country consist of rude jars and bowls, modelled with the hand. The bases are flat, and there are sometimes small "lug" handles. Occasionally there are attempts at decoration; a moulded imitation of plaitwork or of cords, or else a white lime paste smeared over the surface, bearing vertical lines roughly painted upon it in a brownish red. This coloured decoration sometimes washes off in water, showing that it was applied to the vessel after it had been fired. Beginning with this low artistic standard, we can trace a gradual improvement in the shapes and decoration of vessels. The forms become graceful; the painted lines are applied with greater care, and made permanent by firing. The potter's wheel is introduced, and the vessels become more symmetrical in consequence. Large bowls are decorated with painted figures of birds and with geometrical patterns, not very artistically drawn, perhaps, but still showing a striving after artistic effect. There is one type of painted ware which shows bird figures in outline, alternating with spirals and with other devices, and more rarely displaying human or animal (quadruped) figures, which has been considered by recent writers as Philistine ware; but this identification has lately been disputed, and the subject requires further investigation.

With the Israelite immigration there comes, as we have seen, a sudden collapse in civilisation; this is reflected in the pottery as in other handiworks. There is no gradual deterioration; all at once the pottery is found to be coarse and

SPECIMENS OF PALESTINIAN POTTERY OF VARIOUS PERIODS.

ill-made ; the shapes of jars and of bowls lose all the grace which they had possessed ; the painted decoration, such as it was, disappears entirely, or at most is restricted to single lines encircling the vessel. This ill-designed and ill-executed pottery lasts throughout the time of the Hebrew monarchy ; nothing can give a better idea of the low state of general culture during that period.

The pottery of the centuries following the return from Captivity likewise mirrors the involved history of the country. We can easily trace the ever-growing influence of the Hellenic civilisation. However much the Maccabaeans might struggle against Hellenism, they could not keep their followers from preferring the good pot-fabrics of manufacturers trained in Hellenic methods to the wretched native attempts.

Greek painted vases, both red-figured and black-figured, have been discovered in Palestine —or rather, fragments of such vessels have been found, as well as fragments of lecythi. These are, however, by no means great works of art ; the Hellenism that influenced Palestine was of an inferior brand. However, its example has had a salutary influence on the native pottery of the Maccabaean period with regard both to form and to finish. It is baked harder than any earlier ware ; a blind man could distinguish a pile of Hellenistic potsherds from a pile of earlier fragments by striking it with a stick. It returns a distinct musical clink, almost like that of a pile of fragments of china, when thus treated. The surface of the ware is smooth, sends the painted vessels which we have already mentioned. Beside these works of foreign art, the native ware is merely barbarous.

Another interesting study is the development of ornamental patterns. The best scope for such a study is offered by the lamps. In pre-exilic times a lamp was simply a bowl, or a saucer, with a spout pinched out on one side of the rim. The wick lay in the spout, and absorbed the oil with which the saucer was filled. At first the spout projected very slightly, but as time goes on it increased its size; and about the time of the Exile the two lips of the spout had approximated together so that they overlapped. The spout, formerly open, had become a tube. At the same time, the vessel became smaller; and, a little later, to prevent the loss of oil by evaporation, the open surface of the reservoir was closed in, a cover being placed over it with a hole in the middle for filling it. Around the hole and upon the spout there is generally ornament in considerable variety, but, to some extent, capable of seriation into groups. A large *corpus* of illustrations of Palestinian lamps would afford much material for the study of the development of these groups of decorative types.

Especially interesting are the lamps with inscriptions. These date after the time of Christianity, the mottoes being Christian in sentiment. Some are merely inscribed ΛΥΧΝΑΡΙΑ ΚΑΛΑ, " pretty lamp "—a banal motto, though possessing the mild interest of giving us a word that escaped the eagle eyes of Messrs. Liddell and Scott. Others, representing a theology dating after the third century, dedicate themselves to the Blessed Virgin (possibly with a backward glance at the parable of Matthew xxv 1 ff.) by bearing the inscription ΤΗΣ ΘΕΟΤΟΚΟΥ, "of the Mother of God." But the majority of these inscribed lamps bear, or are intended to bear, the inscription ΦΩC ΧΥ ΦΕΝ ΠΑCΙΝ, "the light of Christ shines for all." We say *intended* to bear, for it is only in a very limited number of the lamps that the inscription is at all legible. It is quite clear that the potters themselves were illiterate. They copied the Greek characters by rote, as merely decorative patterns. Naturally, being uncontrolled by knowledge, they distorted the letters to an inconceivable extent, and if we did not know, from the few legible specimens that have come to light, what the inscription was intended for, it would be quite impossible to decipher it on the great majority of these lamps. If we have a long series of these inscribed lamps before us, we can follow the gradual degeneration of the inscription, as copyist follows copyist; now it becomes a mere succession of strokes, now a floral pattern, and now a series of fishes.

Games

The gross amount of time spent in Jerusalem, in any one year, in playing backgammon and similar games is scarcely conceivable. The city suffers from the demoralising influence which is inseparable from the tourist trade. During the

off seven rows vertically and eight horizontally, and then count the number of squares in the rectangle thus defined. Shopkeepers and even bankers in the modern East do not always disdain to aid their arithmetical researches with an abacus. By a rapid and incomprehensible sleight-of-hand they extract from this toy a knowledge of how much change is due to their customer, or what not.

Writing

At the present moment there are three scripts current and official in Palestine: the modification of the Roman script used in writing English, and the native scripts of Arabic and Hebrew. As a visitor walks through Jerusalem he may, in addition, see inscriptions in Russian, Armenian, the Gothic character of German, Greek, and other forms of writing, all testifying to the cosmopolitan character of the city and of its inhabitants.

This has always been the case in Palestine. Many different scripts have been used in the country, and examples of them have been found among the few inscriptions that have come to light from time to time. The Tell el-Amarna tablets, and those found at Taanach, show us diplomats employing scribes who can read and write Babylonian cuneiform. Egyptian kings erect stelæ in hieroglyphs at Beth-Shean, and presumably expect them to be read. The large number of small Egyptian objects which have been found in the country make it probable that intercourse with Egypt was literary as well as commercial.

We know not what script was used during the wilderness wanderings, nor can we say in what characters were written the Tables of the Law, which, whatever their origin may have been, were long preserved in the central sanctuary. In Judges viii 14 we are told a strange thing. Gideon captured a casual boy, belonging to Succoth, and under his orders the boy wrote down for his information a list of the chief men of Succoth. This implies a much wider diffusion of the art of writing than existed under the later days of the Turkish domination. In those days Gideon might have captured fifty boys before he found one capable of writing his own name, let alone those of his neighbours. Either Gideon had remarkable good fortune in finding an accomplished youth, or the proportion of those who could write was greater than in modern times. Such a youth would hardly write in cuneiform; knowledge of that difficult script must necessarily have remained the monopoly of a guild. We must suppose that he wrote in the simple Old Hebrew script, in which Moabite, Phœnician, and Old Hebrew inscriptions are written; in which, indeed, the books of the Bible themselves were first committed to writing.

Until recently the Old Hebrew script was not known to have existed before about the year 1000 B.C. The oldest specimens on record were the Moabite Stone (*c.* 850 B.C.), the inscription on a fragmentary bowl dedicated to

It can have been written only as a display of learning, or as an exercise. The hand is good; the author could write well and neatly. Everything in it points to a well-developed use of penmanship. But we must assume that the vast majority of the contemporary inscriptions have been destroyed; and that most literary works were written upon papyrus, imported from Egypt. Zakar-Baal, king of Byblos, who proved such a formidable host to the miserable Egyptian envoy Wen-Amon, is shown to us in the document describing the adventures of the latter as importing papyrus from Egypt in large quantities, and as keeping regular account-books. But in the damp soil of Palestine no papyrus could be expected to endure to our time. The most that we can hope for are ostraca like those found at Samaria, or the single specimen that has rewarded Mr. Duncan's excavations at Jerusalem.

The Old Semitic script long remained in use in the country. In fact, it still remains there; for the Samaritan community at Nablus even yet make use of it. In tomb and ossuary inscriptions of the first century B.C. we find it giving place to the square script familiar to readers of Hebrew printed books. The change is gradual; sometimes we have inscriptions in a kind of mixed script, compounded of both alphabets. The ossuary inscriptions, which are found in considerable numbers around Jerusalem, offer most valuable material for the palæographic history of the Hebrew alphabet. Ossuaries, as the name implies, are receptacles for bones.

THE GEZER CALENDAR.

Burials took place in chamber-tombs, hollowed at great expense in the solid rock. It would have been quite impossible to provide permanent receptacles for every member of a family to whom such a sepulchre belonged; the tomb-chambers would have had to extend their ramifications indefinitely, as monstrous catacombs, and no purse could possibly meet the cost incurred. Accordingly, it became the custom to provide small limestone coffers, just large enough to contain the bones of a human skeleton bundled together. When a body had decayed, the bones were collected and placed in one of these coffers; the tomb-hollow which the body had occupied thus became free for the next new-comer into the "eternal house." The ossuary boxes were doubtless the work of professional craftsmen; they are made roughly but not unskilfully, and have simple, monotonous, but not unpleasing ornaments cut upon their sides. A favourite device is a circle containing a sex-foil, formed mechanically by stepping a compass from point to point round the circumference. When the box was purchased and the bones were deposited within it, the name of the owner of the bones was often scratched on the side or on the lid of the box. These scratched names are much more roughly executed than the ornamentation, which sometimes it rudely disturbs. They may confidently be attributed to the unprofessional hands of the relatives who transferred the bones to their new receptacle. This makes the inscriptions all the more valuable from the palæographic point of view; they be perceived nearly half a mile off. Nor was there any less primitive way of procuring water than by sending the women of the household to draw it at the village well, often a considerable distance away. The Egyptian water-raising devices, the *sakiyeh* and the *shadduf*, are not unknown in Palestine, but they are not very common; as a rule the water is drawn in bags of hide stretched upon a cross-bar of wood.

In ancient times a drain was sometimes used to carry sewage away to a short distance from the house. It consisted simply of jars with the bottoms broken out, each jar fitting into the mouth of the jar next to it. This makes an improvised pipe, and the matter runs along it to a place where it will either spread over the surface or percolate into the soil as the nature of the ground permits. Formal drains did not make their appearance until the Maccabaean period; we may certainly see in this important and salutary innovation one more debt which Palestine owes to the repugnant West. Several quite elaborate drains, of Roman or later periods, were found by Bliss in his excavations at Jerusalem.

More care was expended upon water supply than on sanitation. The one was a necessity, the other a mere luxury. The great water-tunnels at Gezer and at Jerusalem show that no amount of trouble was considered superfluous in order to provide uninterrupted access to water. It is not clear how the people of Gezer discovered the spring which their tunnel tapped;

THE TOMB OF "THECLA, DAUGHTER OF MARULF THE GERMAN," IN THE VALLEY OF HINNOM.

it was a very strong source of water, rising in a large hollow in the rock which, so far as could be judged, was shut in completely on all sides. The tunnel had to be cut to a vertical depth of over 94 feet to reach the surface of the water. In every town numberless cisterns were hewn out of the rock. But the idea of conveying water into the town from a distance was not formed, or at least given action to, until the time of Herod, among whose grandiose works was the excavation of great reservoirs some six miles from Jerusalem, and the construction of aqueducts to convey the water to stores inside the city. Needless to say, there was no scheme of house service; the water was collected in large open pools, and was drawn thence with pitchers by each family in the usual way.

No doubt there was good reason for *not* establishing aqueducts for conveying water into cities from a distance. In the general disorganisation, and in the total absence of any sentiment of national citizenship, which is obvious throughout almost the whole history, any city could easily cripple a rival by cutting its aqueducts. No community could afford to trust such a vulnerable device. Such interference has happened in quite modern times. Early in the century a rudimentary water supply, on Herodian lines, was installed by the Turks in Jerusalem. The people of Beth-lehem, some five miles away, claimed that they had the right to the water which Jerusalem was thus drawing, and they broke the conduit.

He who would be a social reformer in

numberless cemeteries have been exploited, leaving nothing to science but the empty chambers. Happily there is now some check on this unprincipled trade, thanks to the Archæological Department of the British Mandatory; but in the later years of the Turkish domination, the amount of harm done passes estimation.

Until the tourist-and-museum traffic gave a pecuniary value to earthenware and other previously worthless objects, there cannot have been much reward in work of this sort. Gold was the chief prize at which the earlier robbers aimed; and it is no doubt possible that they found a considerable amount of gold deposited in some of the larger and wealthier tombs, such as the so-called "Tombs of the Kings." But it would be necessary to work long and hard at tomb-robbing to find enough gold to repay the expenditure of time and trouble. Hardly any gold was discovered in any of the tombs opened during the excavations of the Palestine Exploration Fund in the Shephelah. But though the return may have been small, there was always the gambling excitement, which had much to do with keeping the art alive down to the time when it was requickened and systematised by the dealers.

As the grave-goods are therefore lost to us, in the vast majority of cases, the history of tomb-architecture can never be written so fully as might have been the case. We can but do our best with the materials which commercial greed has left us.

The earliest burial-places in Palestine were

natural caves. I have been told of a village in the Lebanon region—I do not know its exact locality—which still uses caves for sepulture. There is a series of these caves in the neighbourhood, which are blocked with large stones. When a death takes place, the villagers open one of the caves and there deposit the corpse. There is a fixed numerical order in which the caves are opened; when the last cave has been used, they begin again with number 1. It is clear that with so crude a method of interment it is quite impossible to preserve any memorial of the deceased; and this reticence has become traditional in Palestine. The Palestinian tomb-explorer returns to his own region from a tour in Egypt with a renewed envy of his colleague whose lot is cast in the latter country. Even where the modern Egyptian has rifled the contents of an Egyptian tomb, he has left, at least in part, the painted decorations with all their varied representations of life in this world and the next, as well as the inscriptions which record the activities of the dead man and his faith in his gods. In Palestine, when the fellah has "scooped" the tomb-deposits, to be sold for a few piastres to the middle-man and then to be dispersed over all the States of the Union and half the countries of Europe, there is rarely left anything but bare stone walls for the explorer to contemplate.

It does not appear that any more shapely tomb was made in the country down to the time of the Hebrew monarchy. So far as any Canaanite tombs have been discovered, they are

village of Silwan could be removed, it is highly probable that other very important tomb-chambers, of the period of the Hebrew monarchy, would be found underneath it.

But it was not until after the Exile that artistically made tombs began to be common. Once more, this was doubtless due to the civilising influence of Hellenism, against which the native purists fought so long and so bitterly. The tombs of the Ptolemaic and Maccabaean period consist of low chambers, entered by means of a square shaft-opening in the roof, through which the person entering drops on to a block of rock rising from the floor to serve as a step. The graves are in a row, of a trough shape, at right angles to the wall as a rule, and are covered with stone slabs. The burial deposits were laid either upon the cover-slabs, or beneath them, on the body. They consist of cheap ornaments, small figures of deities, lamps, and, in one tomb that was opened near Beit Jibrin by the Palestine Exploration Fund, a little pot of powdered lead. This was quite obviously a cheap substitute for the favourite cosmetic antimony (*kohl*) with which the Oriental beauty fondly imagines she enhances her natural charms. Slightly later, it would seem—but the precise chronology is difficult to recover, for reasons already sufficiently given—the bodies were deposited in *kokim*. This is the technical term in the literature of Palestinian archæology for graves in the shape of horizontal shafts driven into the wall at right angles to its plane. In the normal tomb-chamber, there are nine of these shafts, three in each wall except the wall containing the door. The shafts are as a rule just big enough to receive a single body, thrust into them endways. But sometimes they are double, for two bodies side by side ; and sometimes one of the kokim, arbitrarily selected, will be found on investigation to be really a passage, leading to a further chamber which the tomb-excavators had hoped to keep secret.

The most elaborate tomb that has yet been found in Palestine, the sepulchre of Apollophanes of Marissa, is of the kokim variety. In plan it may be compared to a cruciform Church, though the part corresponding to the " nave " is shorter than that corresponding to the " chancel." The " nave " is really a vestibule, through which we proceed by a doorway to a transept, crossing the axis of the excavation, and with kokim opening out of each wall. Another doorway leads from the " transept " to the " chancel," which is a long hall, having kokim on each side. Above the kokim there is a frieze of painted animals, each accompanied with its name in Greek—an elephant, a rhinoceros, a leopard, and so forth. Intermingled with the animals were figures of men—a horseman attacked by the leopard, a trumpeter, a man leading the elephant ; but unfortunately the fellahin, who discovered the tomb, saw in these representations of human beings a violation of the precepts of their religion, and destroyed them. There is also a vigorous painting of Cerberus ; and the inner end wall bears paintings of eagles and vases. The names of the people buried in the kokim have been added as burial succeeded burial, and there are also some curious graffiti ; one, of quite exceptional interest, will be discussed in the following chapter.

A second, and probably later, variety of tomb consists of a chamber with benches parallel to the walls, resembling the berths of a ship's cabin. Such benches are called *arcosolia*. Usually there are three arcosolia in each chamber, one in each wall except that containing the entrance. Some larger chambers have more than one arcosolium in each wall. Arcosolia and kokim are sometimes found together in the same tomb : a good example of this combination is the so-called Tombs of the Judges, north of Jerusalem. Arcosolia sometimes appear in Herodian tombs, as in the well-known Absalom's Pillar ; but as a rule tombs with arcosolia are of Christian date. They are often decorated with crosses. The "Garden Tomb" is a variety of the arcosolium type, in which the bench is hollowed to make a sort of coffin ; but instead of being a rock-cut trough, as in the Maccabaean tombs, the front of the grave hollow is made with a movable slab. One of the slabs had been broken and removed, presumably by the thieves that at some time rifled the tomb ; it would have made a useful paving-slab.

Tombs were sometimes built, not cut in the rock. One of the most remarkable built tombs remaining is at Khirbet Shema, a few miles from Safed. It probably owes its preservation to the great size of the stones of which it is formed. It is hardly to be expected that mausolea built of

THE TELL BARAK SARCOPHAGUS.

small cut stones would survive through centuries of spoliation. No man's tomb was safe whenever the last of his descendants who cared for his memory had joined him in the World of Shadows. A fine sarcophagus of about the second century A.D. was found in 1924 in what was left of such a tomb, at a place called Tell Barak, near Cæsarea. The tomb had gradually been reduced to its foundations by masons taking away stones for building ; to restore its original plan proved an impossibility. But almost by a miracle the sarcophagus had escaped notice, buried as it was in rubbish ; and it was found possible to recover it almost intact. It is now in the Jerusalem Museum.

It is an instructive example of sculpture. Evidently it is a copy, and a clever one, of a good model. On one side there is a lively representation of a combat of Greeks and Amazons, which is carried round on to one of the ends. There is considerable vigour in the composition ; but if examined critically the details are seen to be by no means first-rate. The bodies of the combatants are rather clumsy, their faces poor and conventional—many of them have a strangely Oriental cast of countenance that could be matched by faces to be met with in a walk through Jerusalem of to-day. In some cases the attitudes depicted are so violent as almost to transcend possibility. The opposite side of the sarcophagus has an excellent representation of two gryphons facing one another ; this is by far the most artistic part of the whole work. On the other end a horseman is shown attacking a warrior on foot.

CHAPTER V

EXCAVATION AND RELIGIOUS HISTORY

A NUMBER of years ago an American gentleman — known to the present writer, but now deceased — was fired with an ambition to excavate in Palestine. In order to raise funds for this purpose, he went to interview a wealthy relative, and laid his proposals before him. The relative was, however, cautious. He wanted to know something about his kinsman's ultimate purpose in this undertaking. The other thought to appeal to the known religious sympathies of the man of wealth, by telling him that he hoped " to prove the truth of the Bible " : but he was met with the unanswerable question, " Yes, but suppose you prove the Bible *isn't* true, what then ? "

Both speakers were absurdly wrong in their ideas of the aims and results of excavation. The Biblical record, like any other literary document, must stand or fall on its own merits. It cannot be either authenticated or disproved, as a whole, by excavation. In minor points of detail it can be corroborated, or it can be corrected. For example, the Book of Kings appears to give a date for the rebellion of Mesha which is incompatible with the account of the event recorded for us, on the Moabite stone, by Mesha himself. But even here, if we knew everything, we might be able to see that the two histories are not so irreconcilable after all. For all we know, there may have been two rebellions; there may even have been two Meshas.

What we gain from excavation is illustration, rather than confirmation. Above all, we obtain a background, filling in the outlines drawn by the historian. We learn how to look at the events which the historian describes for us. We learn—and it is a very necessary lesson—not to think of Bethany and its village life as though Bethany were a village in England; we learn not to picture Solomon's Temple in our minds as though it were a building of the impressive immensity of a French Cathedral.

The Bible is the record of the gradual progress made by one favoured community in the discovery of the Divine: beginning with the rudest and crudest savagery, and advancing thence in knowledge until the time was ripe for a fuller revelation, to be made by the mysterious Stranger in Israel who appeared in the land of Palestine nearly two thousand years ago. The book, or rather the collection of books contained within its covers, is thus a manual of the religious history of the people with which it is chiefly concerned; and its record can be illustrated by the results of excavation in the land which that people inherited.

Let us trace in the simplest outlines the course of this religious history. The Israelites entered

read somewhere that the vibrations set in motion in the atmosphere by a spoken word continue to tremble unceasingly ever afterwards. Whether this be true physics or false I know not, and it matters nothing here. The prayers and the songs of ancient Canaanite devotees may even yet be shimmering in the air around us, for all we know. But though it be so, we cannot capture them. It would be rash to prophesy that the already overwhelming marvel of wireless communication may not in some future generation be made retrospective, so as to capture the vibrations of an extemporisation by Bach, a speech by Cicero, a " first night " of a Sophoclean tragedy, a Psalm by David. But such a feat lies still in the realm of fantasy, and for us the Canaanite songs are lost for ever. The green trees under which they performed their rites live only in the pages of the Book which condemns them. Yet they have their descendants in Palestine unto this day ; even now in the villages and on the hilltops there are trees, sacred to the spirit of a Muslim saint that lies buried beneath them, and hung with rags torn from the vesture of devotees. Any instruments that may have been made of wood have perished : writings—like those curious letters addressed to Abraham and the other patriarchs which modern Jews thrust into a crevice in the outside of the mosque alleged to cover the Cave of Machpelah—such have long since disintegrated. A picture of an ancient religion drawn from the scanty materials which a damp climate has allowed to survive the corrosion of three or four thousand years cannot be complete.

The building of Solomon's Temple marked a new departure in Semitic religion. The only temples that are recorded to have existed in the land, prior to the temple of Jerusalem, were those of the Philistine gods mentioned in the Books of Judges and of Samuel, the temple of Baal-Berith at Shechem of which we read in the record of the short-lived reign of Abimelech, and Eli's temple at Shiloh. Shechem was ruled by a clan that was uncircumcised, as we learn from the story in Genesis xxxiv ; that is to say, by a family of non-Semitic origin. Thus the only temples in Palestine earlier than Solomon's, of which we have any knowledge, belonged to non-Semitic people. Quite likely the temple of Shiloh was another such structure, which had been adapted for the housing and cult of the Ark : and most likely the Temple of Solomon was founded on these early models. It had a Philistine guard, as we learn from the story of the slaying of Athaliah in II Kings xi (see the article *Cherethites and Pelethites* in Hastings' *Bible Dictionary* for further references). A building discovered at Gezer was conceivably a small temple with a pillared forecourt ; this city also, it is to be remembered, was within Philistine territory. We have already mentioned the single large building stone found there, which may have belonged to an Egyptian temple.

Save for these individual buildings, the centres of worship in the land were the *High Places* (*bamoth*). To a certain extent we can reconstruct these sanctuaries from the descriptions that have come down to us. A hoary but vigorous tree, hung with rags and with other votive offerings; beside it one or more pillar-stones, which served at once as images and as altars, acting as intermediaries between the material world of the worshipper and the intangible world of the being to whom he addressed his worship; a wooden post, perhaps worked rudely into a human semblance; a well, whence water could be drawn for lustrations and for libations; a tumulus, marking the resting-place of some ancient worthy, whose spirit brooded over the sanctuary and received at least a share in the ritual worship—of these elements, in various combinations, were the Canaanite and early Hebrew High Places made up. Around the whole was a circle of boulders or of standing stones, enclosing the sacred ground, only to be trodden with unshod feet. Such were the places, the rites of which rendered them loathsome to the eyes of the prophets of a pure monotheism. "Nevertheless the High Places were not taken away"—with this stigma is smirched the record even of some of the best of the kings of Judah.

Most likely there were two kinds of High Places in the country. The first kind consisted of the hill-top sanctuaries, often remote from human occupation: the second, of sacred places within the city walls. It is not surprising that centuries of iconoclasm have destroyed all the sanctuaries of the first group. Those lonely shrines were liable to desecration and destruction, whenever religious development had passed the

A HILL-TOP WELY.

stage to which they were appropriate. And yet, though they have perished, we cannot say that their memorial has perished with them. They are perpetuated in the dome-crowned shrines which still stand on the highest hill-tops of Palestine. Probably there is not a landscape in the country which does not include such a sanctuary; a little plain square stone building, the chief interest of which centres in a tomb, as did that of its ancient Canaanite predecessor. Under the strange but thin disguise of a Muslim sheikh some ancient Canaanite spirit of fertility is here still worshipped. A *mihrab* or prayer-niche points the way to Mecca, and the true believer, as he prostrates himself before it, still turns himself toward the ancient pagan fetish, the Black Stone, which has survived the Prophet's assault on the faith of his fathers, and still almost insolently dominates the new faith which he founded.

It is commonly said that objects deposited in these shrines are as safe as if they were in a bank, under the guardianship of the *wely*, the presiding saint of the shrine. Certainly I have seen a man struck with panic at the bare idea of carrying away a pot of excellent olive oil, placed in one of these shrines which I chanced to visit in his company. On the other hand I once left a small coin, worth about a half-penny, in the prayer-niche of a shrine in a remote part of the country not likely to be visited by any but local natives. On returning shortly afterwards I found that in the mean-time the acquisitiveness of some passer-by had other three having been destroyed. The central stone of the seven—that of which the base alone remained—was not quite in alignment with the rest, but was slightly to the north of the line. To the north of it there was a semi-circular wall, the convex face turned toward the stone, the concave face turned toward an apse-like recess in the centre of the northern wall of the square enclosure. These curved walls evidently had some ritual purpose which, in our ignorance of the ancient rites, eludes us. A row of small chambers three or perhaps four in number ran along the south side of the enclosure: there seems to have been a similar row, or perhaps one long chamber, along the north side. The alignment itself ran east and west.

Similar in character, though more imposing, was the alignment of rude pillar-stones found at Gezer. Here there was a group of seven stones, in height ranging from 5 feet 5 inches to 10 feet 9 inches, and a separate group of three stones (two of them reduced to stumps) in the same line, but divided from the others by a wide space. These monoliths stood on a platform of small stones. The surviving member of the group of three was not of the local limestone; it displayed peculiarities of texture which differentiated it from the stone of the district. It has been suggested that this had originally been a sacred stone in the High Place of some rival city, which had been dragged to Gezer as a mark of conquest, as Mesha dragged the "Ariels," whatever these may have been, from

THE PILLAR-STONES OF THE GEZER HIGH PLACE.

a shrine of Yahweh and set them up in his own holy place, as a trophy for Chemosh. In connexion with the pillar-stones at Gezer there were no certainly recognisable sacred buildings remaining; but there were two caves in the underlying rock which, it can hardly be doubted, were an intrinsic part of the sanctuary.

What rites did these hoary pillar-stones witness in ancient times? "The iniquity of the Amorites" is a recurrent phrase; but we should be careful of the sense to be attached to the expression. There is an implication of moral turpitude, of a deliberate choice of evil, in our use of the term "iniquity," which it would be inexact to emphasise in this particular connexion. Doubtless the rites of the High Places would appeal to an individual morally warped. Doubtless they would have a subtly deteriorating effect on the morals of the community at large; the licence which they encouraged, and on occasion even enjoined, would in itself be destructive of personal self-control. But it would be a grave mistake to imagine that they had been deliberately contrived in order to satisfy the lower cravings. They had come into being when the ancestors of the Semites were on the level of savages. It is among folk of low culture that magical practices flourish. As civilisation advances their futility becomes more and more apparent. When civilisation is destroyed, there is a recrudescence of them; the spread of the "mascot" folly in England is an index of the grave deterioration which resulted from the many animals are far superior to their feeble human competitor. No man can draw or carry like a horse ; no man can fully realise a popular simile and swim like a fish. It is not surprising therefore that, below a relatively advanced stage of culture, the life of an animal is conceived as being on a higher plane than the life of a man ; and that primitive folk, as they watch a community of beavers building their dams, should conclude that the whole great world on which we dwell was the handiwork of a creator in the outward form of a monstrous beaver.

Clay statuettes of the divine bull are often yielded by excavation. They are quite as bad, artistically, as the plaques of the mother-goddess. The formless object which resulted from Aaron's ill-omened experimenting with the people's gold—" out came this calf " or, more accurately, this bull—was probably only a vague semblance of the animal. Imagination supplied the rest.

Even the national Deity Himself was conceived of, in early times, under a bull form. It would be the greatest mistake to suppose that the shrines erected by Jeroboam, " who made Israel to sin," were in any sense of the word heathen temples. They were temples of Yahweh, and the bulls which they contained were intended to be representations of the national God. Jeroboam is indeed a much misunderstood individual. He first appears on the scene as a diligent workman. Then he is chosen by a prophet of Yahweh to champion the cause of Yahweh against the foreign cults introduced by Solomon's harim. Next he leads a revolt against the intolerable oppressiveness of the house of David. So far, everything that we hear is to his credit. It was a natural political move—nay, assuming the necessity for maintaining the divided kingdom, it was a necessary political move—to set up shrines to rival the growing prestige of the new establishment at Jerusalem. The latter sanctuary was full of figures of brazen bulls, seemingly without offence: and there is no evidence that to his contemporaries his installation of golden bulls in his own temples was regarded as being any more of an outrage on true religion. He was a conservative rather than an innovator. He worshipped his ancestral God in the ancestral way; and that he was a sincere worshipper of Yahweh, according to his lights, is shown by the fact that his sons bore names compounded with the name of the Deity: and by the further fact that a priest called Amaziah, a name signifying "Yahweh hath been mighty," ministered in his shrine at Beth-el when, in a later century, Amos made his meteoric appearance there, to denounce the vices of king and of court.

It is a familiar truth that some indication of the gradual supersession of traditional beliefs by the uncompromising worship of Yahweh alone may be found in the treatment of the proper names of certain Biblical characters. Saul had no compunction in naming one of his sons "Ish-Baal," that is, "Man of Baal." Later scribes either modify the vocalisation, making a meaningless Esh-baal, or else boldly change the name altogether into Ish-bosheth, which has the improbable meaning of "Man of worthlessness." Another Ish-Baal, one of David's knights, is still further corrupted into Josheb-Bashebeth. Saul's son Jonathan, whose name describes him as "given of Yahweh," and was therefore fully orthodox, had a son whom he called Merib-Baal, "Baal is his champion"; this name is similarly modified to the now better known Mephi-bosheth. It is unnecessary to say here that in these early names, *Baal* and *Yahweh* had practically the same meaning. Not till the mission of Elijah against the worship of the Tyrian Baal did the word begin to appear heathenish in the eyes of the devotees of the Hebrew faith. Previously it was not a proper name at all, but a colourless term signifying "Lord," and capable of being applied to any deity whatever in the country where his authority was recognised.

The collection of ostraca found in the excavations of Samaria give us fresh and valuable material for studying proper names from this point of view. Valuable, because they come to us from the very hands of the owners of the names, or from those in direct relation with them; and not through an indefinitely long succession of scribes and copyists, who introduced such modifications as we have noticed, when their own religious sense was outraged. The documents refer entirely to business transactions in wine and oil. They all fall into three or four stereotyped formulæ, to the effect that in such and such a year, presumably the year of the reigning sovereign, from such a place, so many jars of wine or of oil have been delivered to such a person for the benefit of such another person. It is not quite clear whether these records, written with ink upon broken potsherds, are receipts or invoices; nor are the mutual relations of the recipient and the beneficiary as obvious as they would have been had the writers been more explicit. The meaning of these documents, which are sixty-three in number, is, however, of minor importance; their chief value lies in the names of places and persons. Among the former occur a number of places not known from the Biblical record; such are Shephten, Yetset, Ketseh, Azah, Kerm-ha-Tell, and Beer-Yam, as well as Hazeroth, which can hardly be the place of that name mentioned in the record of the Wilderness wanderings. One or two names of which the reading is doubtful are here omitted; and the vocalisation, which is not indicated in the Old Hebrew Script, is more or less arbitrary. Other names are found in the Biblical text, or rather in *a* Biblical text: it cannot be a mere coincidence that they appear grouped in both documents. In Numbers xxvi 28, Joseph's son Manasseh is said to have had a son Machir; Machir, a son Gilead; and Gilead six sons, by name Iezer, Helek, Asriel, Shechem, Shemida, and Hepher. Further Hepher had a son Zelophehad, who had five daughters, Mahlah, Noah, Hoglah, Milcah, and Tirzah. These names, and their genealogical connexions, are repeated in Joshua xvii 1–3, with the one difference that Iezer is corrected to Abiezer. It is certainly noteworthy that of these twelve descendants of Gilead, the names of no less than six reappear in the list of places which supplied the commodities referred to in the documents : namely, Abiezer, Helek, Shechem, Shemida, Noah, and Hoglah. Especially interesting is the inclusion of Abiezer, in view of the rather contemptuous reference to its vintages in Judges viii 2. This definitely proves the long-accepted contention of critics, that the genealogical names in such passages as these are tribal rather than personal ; and it further teaches us that the sections of the tribe of Manasseh, here enumerated, were settled in a region recognised as a favourable place for the cultivation of vines and olives.

Our special concern in the present connexion is, however, with the personal rather than the local names. Of these about forty-six are legible. Many of these names reappear in the Biblical texts, though naturally not indicating the same personalities ; indeed, some of the forty-six are duplicated on the ostraca and may denote more than one individual. Among already familiar names we may mention Ahaz, Ahimelech, Elisha, Gomer, Sheba, etc. Of the names on the list, ten are compounds of the name of Yahweh : Abiah, Gediah, Jedaiah, Jehoiadah, Shemaraiah, etc. ; and only seven are compounds of the name of Baal : such as Abi-Baal, Baalzamar, Baalmeoni, Merib-Baal. The " seven thousand in Israel " whom Elijah in his pessimistic despondency could not or would not

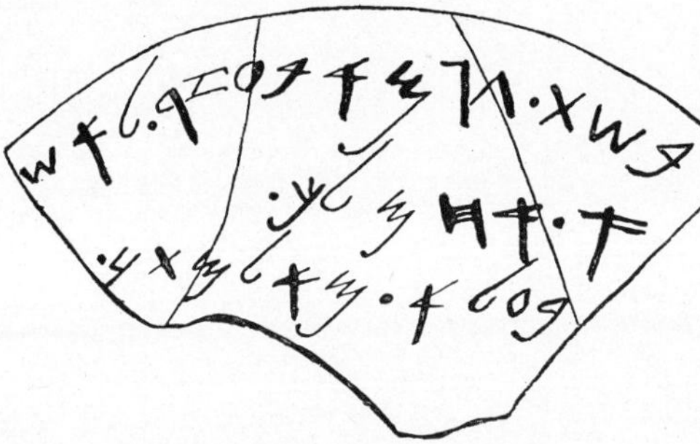

TRANSCRIPT AND TRANSLATION

בשת · ד∧ מאבעזר · לאש-

to-Isha from-Abiezer 14 In-the-year

א אחמלך

Ahimelech

בעלא מאלמתן

from El-Mattan Baala

In the year 14, from Abiezer to [the merchant]
Isha son of Ahimelech, [a consignment of wine for]
Baala who lives at (or comes from) El-Mattan

AN OSTRACON FROM SAMARIA, RELATING TO A TRANSACTION OF THE "VINTAGE OF ABIEZER."

see, may on this proportion have been actually a majority of the inhabitants. A suggestive fact seems to emerge from the scanty material supplied by the ostraca, which may be verified by further discoveries of a similar nature; namely, that Baal-names and Yahweh-names respectively seem to run in families. Baala is a son of Baal-meoni; while on the other hand Gedaiah is a son of Marnaiah, and Obadiah is a son of Abiah (or of Labiah?: the reading is here doubtful). This last person may well be the major domo of Ahab, of whom we read in I Kings xviii; a man in such an office would naturally be concerned from time to time with such transactions as are recorded in the documents. The only other name that might be identifiable is Nimshi, who might quite possibly have been the father of the usurper Jehu.

A specially interesting name is Egeliah son of Elisha (certainly *not* the prophet of that name). Egeliah means "calf" or "bull-calf" of Yahweh. The word *egel* is the word which denotes the Wilderness golden calf, as well as the similar images set up by Jeroboam. Such a name clearly shows that the cult of these objects had not yet fallen into reprobation.

The first to preach against the calf-worship seriously was Hosea; but it seems to have persisted even into post-exilic times. In the latest excavations of Jerusalem certain fragmentary objects were found in stone, which seem to be part of cow-figures with elaborate head-dresses. They belong to the Ptolemaic period. Further discoveries may give us a complete specimen, which will be most instructive: for the present we must suspend judgement upon them.

While the Semite looked with confidence to his gods, such as they were, to give him the boons which he demanded of them, they on their part were not disposed to render their favours for nothing. The man in authority (king, governor, tribal chief, or what not) expected a *bakhshish* in return for his favours. The god was a sort of divine tribal sheikh, who while protecting the interests of his people, yet lived on the tribute which his people paid him. Sacrifice is the essence of Semitic worship. The firstfruits of the fields, of the stalls, of the human home, these are the god's, and they must be devoted to him. The bodies of infants who died immediately after birth, presumably by violence, were deposited in jars and buried in the floor of the Gezer High Place. A cistern-like cutting close by contained large numbers of animal bones, presumably the rejected portions of animal sacrifices. That the sacrifice of children was a rite well known among the Hebrews is illustrated by the stories of Jephthah, and of Abraham with Isaac: that this custom had at one time been actually normal among them is indicated by the provision of the Mosaic Law made for the *redemption* of a first-born child, as of the first-born of an animal such as an ass, which it was not lawful to offer in sacrifice.

A certain jar found buried at Gezer was filled, when unearthed, with a dry yellow powder. The nature of this powder was not determined at the moment, and the jar stood for some days before it was again examined. The powder was found to have turned, in the meantime, from its exposure either to the air or to the hot Syrian sun, to a resinous substance of about the colour and consistency of treacle. Experiment showed that when burnt this gave off a smoke indistinguishable from the fumes of incense; and subsequent chemical analysis showed that it was a substance of the same character. It was most probably used in religious rites; the religious use of incense by the Hebrews is well-known.

The evidence yielded by excavation on the subject of altars and places of sacrifice is not entirely conclusive. A number of isolated blocks of rock, clearly formed artificially by cutting away the sides, have been noted; not only exposed by removing overlying beds of accumulation, but rising from the existing surface of the ground. One such, noted at the site of Zorah many years ago, aroused some interest in view of its possible connexion with the story of the visit of the Angel of Yahweh to Manoah and his wife. But it cannot be confidently asserted that any of these cuttings are actually altars. They may be merely the leavings of quarrymen, who have cut away from their sides the blocks of stone which they required.

Most puzzling among the antiquities of Palestine are the great areas of cup-marked rock-surfaces, which are sure to be found on the underlying rock, in any extensive clearance. We might almost say with but little exaggeration that wherever in the country there is a flat smooth unbroken surface of rock, there is sure to be a great collection of basin-shaped depressions formed upon it. That these are very ancient is sufficiently proved by the high antiquity of the layer of debris which overlies and conceals them. But to what purpose the inhabitants of ancient Palestine expended such enormous stores of energy in forming these hollows we are unable to do more than guess. As a rule there is no traceable order in the disposition of the cups. They are scattered at random ; sometimes there are three or four so close together that they form one composite group ; sometimes one is isolated from the rest. Large basins, about three feet in diameter and perhaps two feet deep, are found associated with little depressions not much bigger than the saucers in a child's toy tea-set. Oval and circular cups, deep and shallow cups, are intermingled, so far as we have any means of determining, at random. Sometimes a channel drains into one of the cups ; sometimes two cups are connected by a channel. Very rarely indeed is a cup surrounded with a concentric ring, as in the bronze age rock-cuttings of northern Europe. Some cups in Palestine are of such a form that a post resembling a scaffold-pole could be fixed upright in them and would stand securely ; and it is not inconceivable that some such purpose was intended by those of this type. Others, however, are too broad and shallow to serve any such purpose. It very frequently happens that cup-marks are found

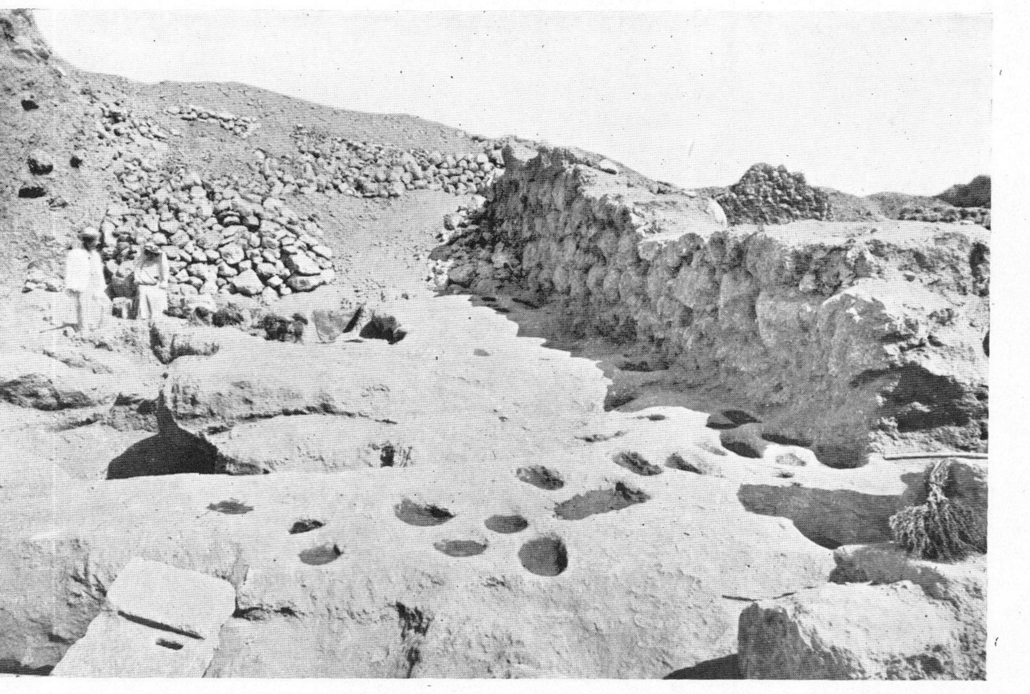

A CUP-MARKED ROCK SURFACE AT GEZER.

on the tops of bosses of rock that rise above the surrounding floor. Cups upon vertical surfaces of rock are of the rarest possible occurrence in Palestine, although they are not uncommon elsewhere, in countries so remote as Scandinavia and India. There were one or two shallow cups on the sides of the standing pillars in the High Place at Gezer. Groups of cup-marks have been found in all excavations that have exposed any considerable surfaces of rock; in all probability they occur under every ancient site. Two of the most noteworthy have been revealed at Gezer and at Jerusalem.

In the impossibility of imagining any use which these cuttings could have served in practical secular life, we are forced to the conclusion that they fulfilled some religious purpose. What that purpose may have been must remain undetermined until we contrive, in some as yet unforeseen way, to obtain much larger knowledge than we now possess on the religion of the ancient Canaanite and pre-Canaanite inhabitants. It is possible that they were for the reception of votive offerings. It is conceivable that a fresh cup was cut on the death of each member of a community, and libations to his ghost were poured into it from time to time. But this is mere guesswork. We can only repeat what we said in introducing the subject, that the vast fields of cup-marks in Palestine present a notable and as yet an insoluble problem.

The raised bosses of rock with cup-marks upon them may possibly have been altars, but of this we cannot be sure. Altars of stone are prohibited to the Hebrews, doubtless because the cutting of such altars would involve the touching of them with the forbidden metal iron. And in fact, the most noteworthy object that has yet been found in the country and that can be called an altar, is the very remarkable earthenware altar of Taanach.

This object, which was broken into thirty-six pieces when it was found, was carefully pieced together, and proved to be a hollow box of terra-cotta 2 feet 11½ inches high, on a base 1 foot 5¾ inches square. The walls of the box are from 1 to 2 inches thick. Toward the top the object narrows; in its summit is a basin-like hollow 11¾ inches across. There is no bottom to the "box," and never has been. It can hardly be doubted that this was an altar for burning incense. The fire was lit upon the ground and the box placed over it. Square holes were left in the front and back of the object, to admit ventilation to the fire, and to provide an exit for the smoke. The incense was placed in the basin at the top, and the fire underneath heated it sufficiently to enable it to give forth its fumes.

Around the basin on the top a number of circles are impressed on the clay; and beneath the edge, on each side, there had been a handle, in the shape of a vertical disc projecting outward from the side and worked on one face into a spiral. This probably was meant to represent a horn. The handle on one of the sides has been broken off, and it was not recovered with the rest of the fragments.

THE ALTAR OF INCENSE, TAANACH.

Below these handles, on each side of the "box," there is a remarkable pile of animal or quasi-animal figures. These are five in number ; they are alternately composite creatures (quadrupeds with wings and with human heads, wearing a sort of cap with dependent tassels) and lions. One of the man-headed figures is just under the handle ; it stands on the back of a lion, which in its turn stands on a man-headed figure, which in its turn is on a lion, below which is a third man-headed figure standing on the ground. It may be questioned whether the maker of the altar intended this piled-up effect to be thus understood by the spectator ; rather are we to suppose that he meant to suggest the altar as being flanked by five beings on each side—a cherub (for the composite beings are probably cherubim) and a lion alternately. On the altar they are represented as in a sort of rude perspective. In addition to these ten figures there is, on one of the sides, behind and above the lower lion, a relief representing a boy or man holding by its neck a snake, which is coiled in a semicircle around him. Low down on the front of the object, between the projecting heads of the lower figures, is another relief, representing a tree, with two gazelles or ibexes leaping up and feeding upon (?) its topmost branches. This device is very obscure and is much injured.

This altar is undoubtedly the most important cult-object which Palestine has as yet yielded. It belonged to a private house ; there was no holy place anywhere near the site which yielded its fragments. Probably it has been broken by the fall of the house in which it stood. It was not of a very high antiquity: the pottery found associated with it, or near it, was certainly of the iron age, and probably of the seventh or eighth century B.C.

A number of fragments, apparently belonging to a second object of the same kind, were found elsewhere in the same mound; but it proved impossible to fit them together.

From the beginning of the colonisation of Palestine the inhabitants, whether pre-Canaanite, Canaanite, Hebrew, Hellenist, or modern Arab, had a faith in the prophylactic power of amulets. The ancient folk who dwelt in the caves of Gezer, before the city was built on the hill, wore goat-bones drilled for suspension. Beads of coloured stone, oddly shaped nodules, crystals, fossils, shells, even the round knob at the articulation of the human femur, all these were collected and perforated for suspension: there was evidently "big medicine" in them. In modern Palestine, practically every one wears amulets of one kind or another; there are many who would probably prefer to go without their clothes than without their amulets, which protect them from every imaginable mischief, from the evil eye to excessive nose-bleeding. Many of the modern amulets are such that they could not be preserved for a very long time—slips of paper with numerical magic squares, gibberish words, verses from the Koran, and the like, written upon them, and sewn inside a small cloth bag. Quite likely this is an ancient custom ; but we cannot expect to find evidence thereof by excavation.

In ancient life, Semitic as well as Indo-European, the house was the temple of the family deities. The hearth was the family altar. The threshold was the entrance to the family sanctuary. It is therefore not surprising that there should be evidence of the sanctity of the chief parts of the house, to be derived from literary as well as archæological testimony. There was a "god" in the door-posts. The ancient covenant law contained in Exodus xxi, whereby a slave is devoted to perpetual servitude, implies this : although the implication is obscured in the two principal English translations, which render the word "the god" as "the judges" and "God" respectively. The same doorpost deity may also be traced in the same document, at Exodus xxii 7. In accordance with this sanctity of the house, we sometimes find evidence of the sacrifice of human beings or of animals at the foundation thereof. At Gezer many cases of the burial of infants under the walls of houses came to light ; and though it is *possible* to explain this as being merely disposals of the bodies of still-born infants, the same cannot be said of the burial of grown persons in a similar situation. At Gezer, Megiddo, and elsewhere, such discoveries have been made. In the recent excavation at Jerusalem the bones of a sheep were found under the threshold of a house whose late date was sufficiently attested by a cross cut on the keystone of the arch that had spanned the entrance. In modern Palestine a sheep is usually killed at the beginning of a house-building.

In many of the ruins of houses unearthed in the tells there has been found a curious collection of pottery objects. These consist normally of a saucer or bowl, in which is laid a lamp, with a second bowl inverted over the lamp. There are, however, many varieties in the number and disposition of the vessels ; but there is always at least one lamp, and at least one bowl. There can be no question that these deposits are in some way connected with rites performed at the beginning of a new building. It is possible that one of the bowls, when it was deposited, contained grape juice or blood, typifying life ; the lamp would be an obvious symbol for fire ; so that the combination was a refinement of the cruder custom of a sacrifice, animal or human. No doubt the original idea was to secure a tutelary spirit that would watch over the new house ; the spirit of the man, slain when it was built, and buried beneath it, would continue to haunt the house and to watch over it. Then, when the advance of civilisation made human sacrifice impossible, animal sacrifice was substituted. By a sacrificial meal the deity whose duty it was to guard the habitation was united with those who were to make use of it. Relics of such rites survive even in modern prosaic civilised Europe. A bottle of wine is broken over a ship at her " christening " (the wine ought to be blood-red, but this is often forgotten). A few coins are sacrificed at a ceremonial stone-laying. They are commonly understood as being corroborative evidence of the date of the ceremony, the coins being chosen as of the date of the current year: but the element of sacrifice comes in even here, for the coins of the current year are usually clean and bright, and are therefore more suitable for sacrifice. I have heard or read somewhere of a pious old countryman who always saved up the brighter and fresher coins that came his way to put into the offertory box on Sundays.

The general result of excavation, so far as pre-exilic religious history is concerned, is to increase our wonder when we read the writings of the Prophets of Israel. That men gifted with a philosophic insight so clear, and with a literary skill so marvellous, should have arisen in a soil so sordid is hardly to be explained otherwise than as a miracle. In the life neither of the people themselves nor of the nations round about, was there any external influence that could have pointed the way beaten out by the pioneer prophets. The pre-exilic Hebrews, as a body, were hardly other than pagan. Their "lapses" into idolatry were not really lapses; they were the normal condition of their religious life. Reforming kings arose from time to time, in every case under the influence of a prophet. Behind the reform of Asa was the obscure Azariah, son of Oded. Hezekiah would have been nothing, had not Isaiah stood at his back; Josiah was moved to his great purge by the discovery of the "Book of the Law" in the Temple. These reforms were never more than temporary. To Hezekiah succeeded Manasseh, who devoted his whole long career to undoing his father's work; while the pages of Jeremiah are eloquent testimony to the ultimate failure of the work of Josiah.

The papyri of Elephantine have cast a lurid light on the religion of the rank and file of the Hebrew people. These documents, which must rank among the greatest discoveries made in recent years, in the countries of the ancient East, relate to the affairs of a Jewish colony, which must have entered the service of the king of Persia shortly before the Exile, and which, at first established as an outpost on the island then called Yeb, at the frontier of Egypt, had there settled down and had entered civil life. The period over which the papyri permit us to watch their proceedings covers most of the fifth century B.C.

Their chief deity was named Yahu or Ya'u, and is no doubt the Yahweh of the Old Testament—the name which, by a succession of misunderstandings, has taken in ordinary English the form "Jehovah." But He was by no means their only god. They had a number of other deities; and these deities bore Semitic, and essentially Syrian names. In other words, these Jews had carried their gods and goddesses with them from the land of their fathers, and had transplanted them to Elephantine. It is most noteworthy that they are *not* led aside to pay homage to the gods of their Egyptian neighbours, except in certain special circumstances. Jeremiah came in contact with Egyptian Jews, at a date rather earlier than the papyri, and was then shocked at their heathen practices ; but they excused themselves on the ground that they were only doing what " they and their fathers, their kings and their princes, had done, in the cities of Judah and in the streets of Jerusalem " (Jer. xliv 27). They were simply maintaining the traditional religion of their forefathers, untouched by reforming king, or prophet, or Mosaic law-book.

Yahu is their chief God ; He is called " *the* God," *par excellence*, or " the God of Heaven," in the papyri. As in the Old Testament, names compounded with His are common ; as we turn the documents over, familiar names catch the eye, such as Zephaniah, Abijah, Azariah, Jonathan, Shemaiah, Isaiah, and others, as well as some that do not happen to appear in the Old Testament such as Mibtahiah, Reuiah, Immanuiah (but compare with the last two Reu-el, Immanu-el, where the common noun " god " is substituted for the divine name). Although chief God, however, Yahu is not supreme, or even unique. Among the documents, there is a list of subscriptions to a certain religious fund. The names of the subscribers are set forth, with the amounts given by each ; the list is as formal as that contained in the report of a modern charity or Church organisation. At the end is a statement of the allotment of the sum collected, which is very instructive ; it runs as follows :—

	kerashin	shekels
The money which was paid into the hand of Yedoniah, son of Gemariah, on the 3rd day of Phamenoth in the Fifth Year [*i.e.* 419 B.C.] was	31	8
Of which		
For Yahu..	12	6
For Ishum-Bethel	7	0
For Anath-Bethel	12	0
	31	6

A *kerash* was equivalent to ten shekels. It appears that two shekels adhered to the palm of Yedoniah, whom other documents show us to have been the leader of the community at the time. These Jews evidently associated two goddesses with Yahu, one of whom obtained almost as great a share of the money subscribed as Yahu Himself. Not improbably this goddess, Anath, or as she is here called, Anath-Bethel, was actually the " Queen of Heaven " against whose worship Jeremiah protested in vain. Jeremiah's own village, Anathoth, had been consecrated to her worship ; its name means " the Anaths " ; in all probability there had been here, in former times, an alignment, or a stone circle, or some similar monument, the component pillars of which were understood to represent the goddess. One of the judges was called " Shamgar son of Anath "—a name so heathenish that some commentators have felt constrained to believe that he was an oppressor rather than a judge. But these papyri show that although there are certain other difficulties in the Shamgar story, into which it would here be irrelevant to enter, his name is no obstacle to taking him for a true-born Israelite.

We may briefly glance at some of the other documents of the series, so far as they throw light on the religion of the community. We number them as they are numbered in the authoritative edition of Cowley.

II. A contract for the supply of barley and beans, dated 484 B.C. It refers to a payment of 100 kerashin of pure silver, to the receipt of which the contracting parties swear "by Yahu the God." The names of these persons (Hosea, Ahiab) show them to be Jews.

V. A document conferring a right to Koniya to build a "portico," whatever the nature of this structure may have been, between his house and that of Mahseiah (471 B.C.). Although this document offers nothing directly bearing upon religious questions, it is very interesting, and gives us much information on the relations between some of the most prominent members of the community. Several of the neighbours of the contracting parties are referred to, and there is sufficient material provided to enable us to draw a sketch-plan of this part of the town, lettered with the names of the occupants of each property. Such a plan has been drawn by Hoonacker, one of the chief commentators on the papyri, and it has been reproduced by Cowley. It teaches us that at the time of the transaction to which the document refers, the Jews and Egyptians of Elephantine were living together on terms of neighbourliness and equality, on occasion signing each other's legal documents as witnesses.

VI. A Persian, named Dargman, renounces his claim to a piece of land, the property of a Jew called Mahseiah (of whom we have heard in the preceding document). The date of this transaction is 465 B.C. Dargman had sued Mahseiah in the court; Mahseiah had sworn an oath "by the God Yahu in Elephantine" that the land was his. This oath by the Hebrew God is accepted by the Egyptian court and by the Persian litigant. The document is thus a striking testimony to the influence enjoyed by the Jewish community, and to the respect which outsiders paid to their religion. It offers further information regarding the topography of the town, helping us to verify the map drawn with the aid of V.

VIII, a conveyance of land dated 460 B.C., refers to the deed of renunciation just abstracted, and gives us some further information with regard to the inhabitants of this region of the city.

XIII, a conveyance of a house, dated 447 B.C., tells us a little more about the same group of properties, and adds the most important information that they were clustered around a "temple of the god Yahu," which is named as one of the boundaries of the property to which this document especially refers. We shall hear again of this temple, noting as we pass that the Jews of Elephantine evidently knew nothing of, or at any rate disregarded, the Deuteronomic law of the single sanctuary. Under the shadow of the temple was the house of an Egyptian whose name is lost, but who is described as " priest of Khnum and of Sati "—two Egyptian deities.

XIV, dated 441 B.C., is another deed of renunciation. Pi, son of Pahi, renounces his claim to certain property belonging to a woman named Mibtahiah, daughter of Mahseiah. Reading between the lines we can see, though it is not actually stated, that Pi and Mibtahiah have been married, and are now being divorced. Mibtahiah has adopted her husband's Egyptian gods with himself, and in the court she swears, not by Yahu as her father had done, but by the goddess Sati, although she bears so Yahwistic a name (" confidence of Yahweh " or some such meaning). It is noteworthy that there are no Jewish witnesses to this document. Mibtahiah's denaturalisation is not approved by her kinsfolk. These are signs of the beginning of a cleavage, destined to become acute as time goes on.

The matrimonial adventures of this Mibtahiah were rather complicated. She was the assignee of the property specified in the conveyance VIII. She was then the wife, probably newly married, of one Jezan, or Jezaniah, son of Uriah. This was in 460 B.C. By another conveyance (IX) written at the same time, Jezaniah is given the usufruct of the property, but is restrained from the right of sale, in the interests of the children of the marriage. Jezaniah had, however, dropped out by 447 B.C., when Mahseiah, the father of Mibtahiah, settled another property upon her, ignoring Jezaniah, who is presumably dead. She now marries Pi, whom we find divorcing her in 441 B.C., in the document before us. In the same year she married another Egyptian, As-Hor, son of Zeho, by whom she had two sons called by the Jewish names Yedoniah and Mahseiah. In later documents these youths appear described as sons of *Nathan* and Mibtahiah; it would appear as though she had returned to the fold of Judaism, and had carried her new Egyptian husband back with her. The marriage contract of As-Hor and Mibtahiah is extant (XV), with a long list of the valuable gifts which the infatuated bridegroom bestowed upon her. At the time of this third wedding she can scarcely have been in her *première jeunesse!* Among other concessions As-Hor renounces the right of taking to himself a second wife. He did not enjoy his happiness for long; certainly he did not survive to see his sons grow up to man's estate. In XX we read of an action taken against the two young men, in or about 420 B.C., for the recovery of goods that had been deposited with As-Hor, their father. Although he was an Egyptian, the two young men are described as "Jews."

XLIV. This document is undated; it is probably older than 419 B.C., but not much. Meshullam, son of Nathan, sues Menahem, son of Shallum, for half of the value of a she ass, at the moment in the keeping of P[. . . son of Espe]met.* Meshullam's father, who is now

* The fracture in the papyrus can be partly filled with the help of some of the other documents.

called "Pamisi," has asserted that he owns the half-share, having given to Menahem a he ass in exchange for it. Menahem swears *by the God Yahu, by the Temple, and by Anath-Yahu*, that this is not the case. Incidentally we have here another case of proselytism; an Egyptian assuming a Jewish name, though not wholly renouncing his old one, as in the case of Mibtahiah's third husband. But the important point for us in this document is the threefold oath taken by the unquestionably Jewish Menahem, son of Shallum, son of Hodaviah; by Yahu, by the temple, and by a goddess, Anath, who for him is associated with Yahu on equal terms.

XXI. In the year 419 B.C. a bombshell burst on the community. One Hananiah suddenly appeared in Egypt, backed by credentials from King Darius; and in the name of the king he sent a peremptory order to Yedoniah, the head man of the Jewish community, to keep the Passover. Moreover, he instructs him how to keep it. In wonderment, we ask ourselves, had these Jews never kept the Passover before? Did they not know the appropriate ritual? And what had King Darius to do with the matter?

These questions cannot yet be answered. No satisfactory solution is forthcoming for the enigma which this letter presents. But we cannot fail to see a most remarkable parallel between this mission of Hananiah and that of Ezra, some forty years earlier, to the Jews of Jerusalem. Both come under the direct patronage of a king of Persia. Both come to what we may describe, if the colloquialism be permitted us, as a happy-go-lucky community, which sees no harm in such matters as mixed marriages. Both come to establish a more rigid exclusiveness, and a firmer adhesion to what they understand to be the National Law and the National Cult. And both involve the community, to which they come, in suspicion, dislike, and ultimate disaster. It was about the same time, and possibly as a result of the mission of Hananiah, that the subscription list already referred to was opened. It might be that its purpose was to pay for the great feast which had thus been commanded. But Hananiah had clearly not succeeded, any more than his predecessor Jeremiah had done, in putting a stop to the worship of gods other than Yahu. Nay, even he, in addressing Yedoniah, uses the current formula, "May *the gods* seek the welfare of my brethren."

XXV. A document of 416 B.C., relating to the temporal affairs of the family of the ubiquitous Mibtahiah. It is only important for us as evidence that the Temple was then still standing; it is used here as a landmark. But its days were numbered. In or about 410 serious trouble begins to fall on the Jewish community.

XXVII is a complaint to the Persian satrap that the Egyptian priests of Khnum, and the local Persian Governor Waidrang, had turned upon them, stopped their well, prevented their offerings of sacrifices, and looted their temple. But this was only the beginning of the disasters of the community. The Jews were still powerful enough to own property, including slaves; nay, as we learn from XXVIII, written shortly after the petition just mentioned, they could even own Egyptian slaves. This is a contract made between the two sons of Mibtahiah, now deceased, dividing their mother's slaves. These slaves are a woman named Tebo, and her three sons, Petosiri, Belo, and Lilu. They are tattooed with marks that indicate them as being Mibtahiah's property. Yedoniah takes Petosiri, Mahseiah takes Belo; they agree not to divide Tebo and Lilu at the moment, but will later come to an agreement as to their proprietorship. They are evidently still looking forward to an undisturbed continuance in the enjoyment of their goods and chattels: an anticipation fated to disappointment.

XXX. In 408 B.C. we find another petition being presented by Yedoniah on behalf of his community. They had got little satisfaction out of the Governor of Egypt on the former occasion; accordingly they now apply to Bigvai, Governor of Judea. They give a much fuller account of the proceedings of the Egyptian priests and of Waidrang than we can gather from the fragmentary petition XXVII. It appears that the priests went to Waidrang, and petitioned that he should remove the temple of the god Yahu in the fortress of Yeb. Waidrang sent orders to his son Nephayan, commander of the garrison at Syene (Assouan, on the mainland opposite Elephantine), to destroy the temple. (It would naturally not be good policy for Yedoniah to tell Bigvai the cause of this sudden act of hostility against a sanctuary

Heaven in its place as it was before, and let them offer the meal offering and incense upon the altar as heretofore." The Persian could not bring himself to sanction animal sacrifices, which would defile the sacred element, fire, with the contact of a dead body. A fragmentary draft of an answer to this reply (XXXIII) shows the Jews ready to accommodate themselves to the prejudices of their rulers, and undertaking that there shall be no animal sacrifices in the new temple.

But the new temple was never built. A much injured letter (XXXIV), written shortly afterwards (about 407 B.C.), refers to a raid on certain houses in Elephantine, by whom does not appear, and the taking prisoner of Yedoniah. Another letter, of a date a little earlier (XXXVIII), although we cannot say more than that it must be later than 419 B.C., written by a certain Mauziah, throws a faint gleam of light upon the sudden hostility which the Jewish community had aroused. Mauziah recommends to the good offices of Yedoniah two Egyptians, by name Zeho and Hor. Mauziah had got into trouble; Waidrang, the Governor, had cast him into prison in Abydos, on account of some injudicious transaction with a precious stone, which, he delicately mentions, had been found, stolen, in the hands of dealers. Zeho and Hor had succeeded in procuring his release. Yedoniah is given a strong hint that it would be well to keep on the right side of Zeho and Hor; for, as he bitterly complains, "since the mission of Hananiah, Khnum has been against us." It is almost an echo of what we read in the pages of Jeremiah: "Since we left off to burn incense to the Queen of Heaven, and to pour out drink-offerings unto her, we have wanted all things, and have been consumed by the sword and by the famine." Mauziah thinks that he would not have paid the penalty of his rascality had not Hananiah separated out the community to which he belonged as a peculiar people, marked and conspicuous. It was never safe to be conspicuous in the ancient world.

A few other documents remain, which cannot be certainly dated, and which have but little bearing on our present subject. But there is every probability that the raid described in XXXIV was the beginning of an end, which came abruptly and with violence.

The deities, especially of the goddesses, of these Elephantine Jews seem to have been a little vague. We read in one document of Anath-Yahu, in another of Anath-Bethel. Such compound names are not uncommon in Semitic texts. Mesha devotes the spoil of Nebo to Ashtar-Chemosh, a form exactly parallel to the Anath-Yahu of the Elephantinians.

A curious action was taken in the year 461 B.C. (VII). Malchiah, son of Joshibiah, sued a Persian, Phrataphernes, son of Artaphernes, for a peculiar form of slander. Phrataphernes had boasted, apparently falsely, that he had forcibly entered the house of Malchiah. Malchiah sued Phrataphernes for the implied slight on his neglect of his duties as a householder, and the court adjudged that Phrataphernes should swear by the god of Malchiah that he had not committed the action in question. Accordingly, Malchiah causes Phrataphernes to make oath to this effect; but notwithstanding his Yahwistic name, he dictates an oath, not by Yahu but by Herem-Bethel. Both Herem and Bethel appear in personal names among the community; beside the orthodox El-Nathan and Jonathan, "the gift of God" or "of Yahweh," we have Herem-nathan and Bethel-nathan. We have seen the goddess Ishum-Bethel receiving a minor share of the Temple funds; this name has been happily compared with *Ashima*, translated "the sin" of Samaria in Amos viii 14. Other personal names compounded with those of minor deities appear in the earlier documents, but they tend to disappear after the mission of Hananiah.

It may be thought that we have lingered unduly long over these interesting papyri, seeing that they were not found in Palestine. But they are so illuminating, they throw so vivid a light on what the reformers of the Hebrew people were "up against," that they call for the most careful study. We cannot wonder at the rigid exclusivism of the apostles of monotheism, whose names are writ large in the roll of honour of the Old Testament. Nothing short of the consecration of the nation as a peculiar people could have rooted out the Anaths and the Ishums, who stood between the people and the one God of Heaven. We cannot feel surprise at the painful cleansings and lustrations, which by Christ's time had degenerated into mere empty forms; or at that stern inscription which stood at the door of the Temple court, warning strangers who came from the impure lands of impure worships from defiling by their presence the holy sanctuary of Yahweh. This inscription we still may read; and we may still feel something of the thrill that it must have caused to those who read it while it was still set up in its appointed place, two thousand years ago:

LET NO STRANGER ENTER
WITHIN THE BALUSTRADE
AND THE ENCLOSING WALL
SURROUNDING THE SANCTUARY
WHOSOEVER MAY BE CAUGHT
ON HIMSELF SHALL BE THE
BLAME FOR HIS CONSEQUENT
DEATH

We feel that the drafter of the inscription, although his Greek is a little clumsy, had a sense of literary effect. He withholds the dread word ΘΑΝΑΤΟΝ "death," and brings it in at the very end, with an emphasis which shows that he thoroughly meant what he says.

But the efforts after rigid purity were not wholly successful. It is a singular experience to visit the synagogues of Galilee after having read of the Maccabaean fight against Hellenism and the bold stand made against the infusion of Jewish orthodoxy with Classical art. The synagogues of Galilee are structures that were erected in or about the second or third century A.D., after the destruction of Jerusalem and the expulsion thence of the Jews had moved the centre of gravity from the Holy City to Tiberias. They are now almost ruined to their foundations, the most complete relics being the façades of the synagogues of Kefr Berim and of Meiron. Altogether there are remains of about a dozen of these structures extant. They are all built to one plan: an oblong building surrounded on three sides with an aisle, having three doors in the fourth side, one in the middle and one at each end of the aisle. This fourth side, which is one of the narrow ends, almost always faces south.

The buildings are constructed, or at least faced, with well-cut stones, which has made them tempting quarries. A fine doorway of a second synagogue which once stood at Kefr Birim has been utterly destroyed, since it was first described and figured in the Palestine Exploration Fund's Memoirs.

The special point to notice about these buildings is, that in architectural detail they are nothing but clumsy imitations of Roman models. Square lintelled doorways with heavy mouldings surrounding them; sometimes a circular arched tympanum over the door—these are the principal architectural features that strike the beholder. In the ornament and symbolism there are naturally certain specifically Jewish details, such as the seven-branched candlestick, the pentacle, interlaced triangles, and inscriptions in square Hebrew characters. One such inscription, at Nebratein, is of unusual length; but it is so badly carved, evidently by an illiterate stone-mason, working unintelligently from a written

THE FAÇADE OF THE SYNAGOGUE OF MEIRON.

model, that it is utterly impossible to read it. Nevertheless, these Jewish accretions hardly remove the impression that we are looking at degraded Roman buildings.

This, however, is not the most remarkable fact that attracts attention. Most surprising is the free use of animal forms, human forms, and even of heathenish mythological figures in the sculptured decoration. In many cases these have been intentionally defaced—quite as likely by Muslim as by Jewish orthodoxy. Two figures support a wreath in the middle of the lintel of the principal door of the synagogue of Kefr Birim. But it is at Kerazeh (Chorazin) that the most astonishing examples of this style of ornamentation are found. The synagogue here was built with Corinthian columns. It is constructed out of a very hard stone, which, while putting difficulties in the way of artistic execution, has also prevented wilful destruction. On the walls of this singular synagogue there are animals, birds, swags of foliage, genii, and strange composite figures like centaurs. Animal figures also appear in the decoration of the synagogue of Talhum (Capernaum).

The Romanisation of Jerusalem naturally introduced Western paganism into the city. Eusebius tells us, for what it may be worth, that a temple of Venus had been built over the site of the Holy Sepulchre. But this and all other temples that may have been in existence in and around the city have disappeared, save in so far as some of their columns may have been adapted for later churches and other buildings. Naturally such structures would not be allowed to remain as temples after the triumph of Christianity. We have spoken of the votive tablet to Jupiter Sarapis which exists, built into the modern "Zion Gate." A mutilated statue of a deity was found near Gaza by fellahin many years ago; it was probably a piece of local work modelled upon a classical statue of Zeus or of Jupiter. The cleansing of Gaza from pagan deities, and the destruction of the local temple of Marna, is graphically told in the all too short biography of Bishop Porphyrius by the deacon Marcus. The utter destruction of the temple of Marna, which seems to have been a building with no small pretensions to architectural impressiveness, and which only missed reconsecration as a Christian church, and consequent preservation, by a slender chance, is there narrated with a vividness not often found in early ecclesiastical biographies. It may be taken as typical of similar destructions elsewhere in the country.

There remain two important matters that have to be considered briefly before we can claim to have adequately treated the subject of this present chapter. These are (1) the beliefs regarding the state of the dead; and (2) the practices of magic.

It is commonly said that the Hebrew anticipation of the other world was singularly hopeless. Isaiah, some of the chief Psalmists, the great poet who wrote the drama of Job—these express no prospect other than a bloodless,

STONE BEARING A CARVING OF A LION, FROM THE SYNAGOGUE OF CHORAZIN.

emotionless Sheol, dragging its weary monotony through all eternity. True, the last-named author seems to have had occasional stirrings of an instinct that there must be something better in store, where wrongs shall be righted; but they are vague and feeble, and are easily smothered by the intolerable troubles which, in the person of his hero, he represents himself as suffering. If we read the Old Testament record with close attention, however, we shall see that this description of the Hebrew conception is not the whole truth. Alongside with the idea of Sheol, there are traces of others of a more primitive description, which assign to the dead an active interest in the affairs of the living, not always to the advantage of the latter. It can scarcely be from a mere Sheol that the necromancer summons Samuel to speak the word of doom to Saul. Some of the mourning rites that are prohibited in the Deuteronomic legislation most certainly presuppose a belief in the continued activity of spirits of the dead, and an acknowledgment of their existence almost amounting to worship. The process of execution *by stoning* was assuredly followed, in order that the ghost of the dead should be enclosed at once in a great carn, that would effectually shut it in and prevent it from wreaking its vengeance upon those who had deprived it of its life on the earth: compare the heaps of stones erected over notorious malefactors such as Achan and Absalom. Even the Book of Deuteronomy, for all its monotheism, cannot abrogate the ancient rite of the sacrifice of the red heifer, to appease the wrath of one whose blood has been shed unavenged ; parallels from all over the world may be brought into comparison therewith to explain it.

In short, there must have been something more vivid than Sheol in the natural beliefs of the Hebrew people about the life after death. The pre-prophetic Hebrew feared, fed, even worshipped the dead. So well recognised was the custom of making food-offerings to the dead, that the Deuteronomic legislation obliged a man, in paying his tithes, to swear that he had not offered any part of them to the dead (Deut. xxvi 14). We must infer that the doctrine of Sheol was an artificial teaching, devised, adopted, and proclaimed by the prophets, expressly for the purpose of securing that Yahweh should have no rival whatever in the worship of His people. The traditional beliefs of the Hebrews as to the dead were utterly heathenish ; they had to be destroyed before purer and more spiritual beliefs could take their place.

The archæological evidence is in accord with this interpretation of the literary evidence. There would be no point in leaving, with the dead, offerings of food, pottery, ornaments, weapons, and so forth, such as we may find at all stages of the history of Palestine, in the rock-cut tombs that were described in the previous chapter, if the dead were to have no other prospect than Sheol. They must have been expected to have a use for these things.

While we may most conveniently consider

here the evidence of excavation regarding magical practices, we must remember that the study of magic is not properly a part of the study of religion. Rather is it the opposite, the negation of religion. The magician seeks to force the Higher Powers, whatever they may be, to do his will; the religious man recognises the superiority of the same Powers to himself, and his impotence in their presence. Magic is an attitude of revolt, religion of submission. The boons which the magician would wrest from the Higher Powers are many and various: fertility of crops; healing in sickness; foreknowledge of the future; destruction of enemies—these and the like does he seek to attain by spells, or by dramatic and other actions of various kinds.

Although this rigid contrast may be drawn between religion and magic, the two can for a time co-exist in the same nation or person. It is necessary even for the religious man to have acquired a certain degree of spiritual insight, to realise fully the futility of seeking to coerce the divinities whom he worships. In the rude and barbarous days of Joshua and of Saul, it would seem quite natural to force the Divinity to reveal His will, by drawing a pebble of one colour or another from a bag, after a religious ceremony by which an agreement was made with the Deity as to the interpretation to be attached to each. The lot called "Urim and Thummim" does not appear to have been any more recondite than this. Nay, even so late as the time of the beginning of the Acts of the

Apostles, we find Matthias chosen by lot to fill the place of Judas Iscariot, after a prayer for guidance.

As in Egypt and Chaldea, dreams were in Palestine a recognised channel of communication between Deity and man. But not every one could interpret his own dream; one skilled in the science had to undertake the duty. When the priests had laid some unhappy transgressor under an interdict, they could refuse to work any oracle for him: this happened to Saul, and in his desperation he sought to obtain by illegitimate means the wished-for knowledge of the secrets of the future. That there were many irregular practitioners like the witch of En-dor may be inferred from the strict suppression of such persons enjoined in Deuteronomy, with the long enumeration there set forth of the different classes of diviner (Deut. xviii 10 ff.). Foreign, especially Philistine, oracles were on occasion pressed into the service of anxious inquirers, as we learn from the beginning of II Kings, and from an early prophecy of Isaiah (ii 6). From these and similar texts we derive the impression that the whole populace was a prey to charlatans, who, using strange ventriloquial voices, pretended to force the ghosts of the dead to illuminate the dubious paths which in those uncertain and insecure times the living were compelled to walk. Even a Samuel was liable to be called upon to give clairvoyant information as to the whereabouts of lost asses, in return for a trifling fee.

Where such superstition regarding divination prevailed, there was fertile soil for other weeds of Magic. We have already referred to some of them on previous pages of the present chapter: to the wearing of amulets; and to the rites of the High Places, which were much more magical than religious. The strange water-ordeal for testing chastity (Numbers v) is a singular survival of a very primitive form of judicial magic; and the magical power of a curse is well illustrated by the story of Micah (Judges xvii), who restored the silver which he had stolen from his mother, after he had been terrified by the curse which she had pronounced upon the unknown thief.

This leads us to the subject of injury of an enemy by magic, of which we have had direct evidence from the excavation at Tell Sandahannah. One of the most curious discoveries there made was a series of small leaden figures of men, which had been maltreated in various ways—mutilated, or else bound with strips of metal resembling thongs. There can be no question that these figures were magical in their purpose: they were representations of the enemies of the person or persons who made them, and they expressed the hope that, as the figures were misused, so in like manner would those whom the figures represented suffer in their bodies. The superstition is world-wide. A man's portrait is a part of himself; it has some subtle connexion with himself and injury to the portrait is sure to be followed by a corresponding injury to the person.

In another part of the mound there were found fifty-one tablets of limestone, of which forty-nine were inscribed in Greek or in other languages. Most unfortunately these were very fragmentary, and for the greater part illegible; but enough remained to show their nature. They were imprecatory tablets, such as are not infrequently found laid up in ancient temples and other sacred places. A person who has suffered a grievance, writes on a tablet of limestone or (much more frequently) of lead, a prayer that some punishment will befall the author of the injury; he deposits it secretly in the place where the god addressed will read it; and then he departs, assured that he will be avenged in the manner which he suggests. Thus, one Pankles, dwelling in Marissa, had been suffering from headaches, which had compelled him to resign his situation in the service of a certain Demetrius. For some reason he had persuaded himself that Philonides and Xenodicus were responsible for this misfortune; they had worked magic upon him, and caused his malady. He therefore in his turn curses them; may they be deprived of speech and of the pleasures of love! Another tablet has a pathetic inscription upon it. A certain Adam, who is also called Zebatos, writes from a prison where he has been confined for three years. Theon has distrained his goods; he was unjustly treated at his trial, and is now suffering hardships; he is continually being beaten and tortured, and feels himself near to death; let the god hasten, if he is to be delivered, and let him soften the malice of

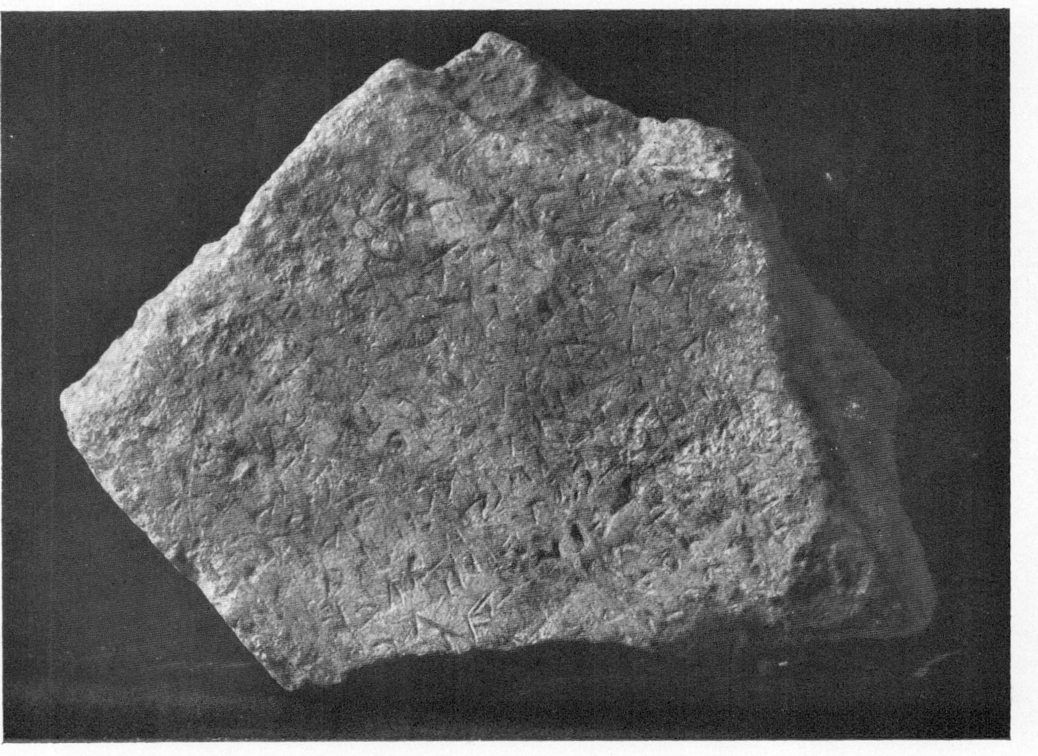

THE TABLET OF PANKLES.

his enemies. Another tablet in the group invokes injuries against one who has appropriated a trust deposited with him, and has committed perjury in connexion with it; another hopes that the person named will die within five days; others curse the marriage, or the heart and the hands, of the enemy.

These cursing tablets were very serious in their intention, and they were very really believed in. If the persons named upon them were aware of their existence, they would suffer many an unhappy hour: quite probably they would have actually induced some of the very evils invoked against them, merely by fretting and worrying over them. It is indeed likely that the magic sometimes actually took effect in this very way, thereby confirming the general belief in its efficacy. But it was not necessary to make a model of the enemy, or to write his name on a tablet. If the worker of magic could obtain something that had belonged to his intended victim—a garment, let us say—he had in his hands ample material for working his wicked will. From the treasury of *The Golden Bough* I quote just two illustrative examples. "The witch in Theocritus, while she melted an image or lump of wax in order that her faithless lover might melt with love of her, did not forget to throw into the fire a shred of his cloak which he had dropped in her house. In Prussia they say that if you cannot catch a thief, the next best thing you can do is to get hold of a garment which he may have shed in his flight; for if you beat it soundly, the thief will fall sick."[1] These—especially the citation from Theocritus—are sufficient to explain to us a strange and suggestive inscription scratched on a door-jamb in the tomb of Apollophanes.

We have explained above that this tomb is in shape like a cruciform Church, the "chancel" and "transepts" of which contain burial-recesses. At the time when the inscription was cut, the "chancel" must have been already in use for interments, shut off from the rest of the excavation by a temporary door. The outer part of the tomb was still empty—perhaps its excavation was not yet completed—and it was accessible to passers by. The inscription referred to is on the right-hand jamb of the door-way as you enter the "chancel"; it must have been just outside the temporary door that at the time shut off access to the place where the dead of the family of Apollophanes were already taking up their last abode. On the opposite jamb is an obscure scribble which seems to make ribald allusion to our inscription, though the sense is hard to understand. If this be a real reference, it gives us the names of the authors of the inscription which we are to discuss as Myron "the priest," and Calypso. If only for convenience we may adopt these names.

The inscription, which is in four lines of Greek, remains absolutely unintelligible, until we notice that, although the handwriting is fairly uniform in general character, there are yet slight differences in the formation of certain

[1] "The Magic Art" (Part I of Frazer's *The Golden Bough*), vol. i. p. 206.

THE DIALOGUE OF MYRON AND CALYPSO.

letters, sufficient to show that it is the work of different writers. It is, in fact, a dialogue. We learn that Myron and Calypso were two lovers, who had probably used the still open tomb-chamber as a secret place of meeting. One or other, or both, must have been of the kindred of Apollophanes, so that occasional visits to the tomb would not cause remark. But in the ancient as in the modern East, a woman was not free to choose her husband for herself; Calypso was forced, unwillingly, into a marriage with some one else. She could not communicate directly with Myron; but she found an opportunity of visiting the old trysting-place, and of scratching on a conspicuous part of the wall the following words:

"There is nothing that I can suffer for thee, or wherein I can give thee pleasure. I lie with another, though greatly loving thee."

In time Myron found this pathetic message of farewell. We can hardly believe that he was really worthy of Calypso's love, when we find that he was capable of answering her thus:

"But by Aphrodite! I *have* great pleasure in one thing: that thy cloak lieth—in pawn."

Poor superstitious Calypso! It is hard for us to imagine her terror when she read this horrible sentence. The heartless, spiteful banter with which he twists her own expressions to suit his meaning could hardly fail to give her pain: and the reference to the cloak must have frightened her out of her senses. We need not pause to speculate in which of many possible ways Myron had obtained possession of this garment. It is quite likely that he had jested with her about the power which it gave him over her, in the days of their association together. He seems to have been a priest, and therefore skilled in magic. In her belief there was absolutely no limit to the capacity for evil, to herself or to her husband, which the possession of the cloak had put in the hands of her former lover. We can see something of her feelings reflected in her handwriting. Her first sentence had been written across the soft limestone surface of the wall in a bold straight line. Myron's answer droops downward to the end of his line—it is hardly too imaginative to see the character of the man reflected in the badly aligned sentence. Now Calypso has not the heart to correct this fault; her new line droops also, though not quite to the same extent; and no wonder, for this is what she writes:

"But I run away, and leave thee plenty of room. Do what thou wilt."

"I run away and leave thee plenty of room," must simply mean, "I go from thee as far as possible." But whither? Could any distance transcend the limit over which magic can act? And how *can* she run away—she, a newly-wedded wife in the harim of some citizen of the town? There is one possible answer to these questions, and only one. She will kill herself, and then he may do his worst!

And it is greatly to be feared that she carried

out her threat. When Myron returned to the tomb he found, in addition to Calypso's last words, a fourth line, written in a strange hand, to this effect:

"Strike not on the walls; it makes a noise. Through the doors she lieth—with ghosts."

The intruder writes in the character of one of the buried dead, protesting against their rest being disturbed by Myron's demonstrations. He was doubtless a Semite, and not an accurate Greek scholar: he misspelt the word for "ghosts," writing instead the word for "nods" (ΝΕΥΜΑCΙ for ΠΝΕΥΜΑCΙ), and thus preparing a pitfall for future interpreters. The emendation is due to the late Colonel Conder: it did not at first appeal to me, but I now see that it is the only possible way of extracting any reasonable sense.

Myron, at any rate, was not misled. He understood, and departed without a word. Let him mumble his spells over Calypso's cloak to his heart's content! In the grim words of the unknown stranger, he would only make a noise. Behind the doors of the tomb she was safe from the evil with which he would have requited the love that she so freely gave him. And let him realise that the "noise" has been heard; that the thing is known; that though Calypso may be dead, her husband is alive, eager for revenge!

But this end of the drama is hidden from our eyes. Shadows have flitted for a brief moment across our vision, only to mingle once again with the mists of the centuries.

out for them. When Mauro repaired to the tomb he found, in addition to [illegible], a fourth [illegible] in a strange hand, to this effect:

"Strike not on the stone; it makes a noise.
Through the doors she flits—with ghosts."

The intruder writes in the character of one [illegible] play [illegible] by Mauro's [illegible]. He was doubtless a genius, and not an accurate Greek scholar; he misspelt the word for "ghosts," writing instead the word for "seeds" [illegible] a pitfall for future interpreters. The explanation is due to the late Colonel [illegible]; it did not at first appeal to me, but I now see that it is the only [illegible] sense.

Mauro's [illegible] was not [illegible]. He [illegible] without a [illegible]. Let him mumble his spells over [illegible] to [illegible]. In the dead watches of the night [illegible] he would only make a noise behind the doors of the tomb [illegible] which would have [illegible] that she [illegible]. And [illegible] had been heard; [illegible] the tomb [illegible].

But this end of the [illegible] is hidden from [illegible] [illegible] for [illegible] [illegible] of the [illegible].

A SHORT BIBLIOGRAPHY

(This is not meant to be a Bibliography of Palestine as a whole, but of the excavations that have formed the basis of the foregoing work.)

Jerusalem

WARREN, CHARLES: Underground Jerusalem.

—— —— Recovery of Jerusalem.

PALESTINE EXPLORATION FUND: Memoirs of Survey of Western Palestine: volume relating to Jerusalem.

BLISS, FREDERICK JONES, and ARCHIBALD CAMPBELL DICKIE: Excavations at Jerusalem, 1894–97. Palestine Exploration Fund, 1898.

VINCENT, HUGUES: Jerusalem sous terre.

WEILL, RAYMOND: La cité de David. Paris, Geuthner, 1920.

Memoir on Excavation in Jerusalem 1923–25. Palestine Exploration Fund, at present (1925) in preparation.

Tell el-Hesy (Lachish)

PETRIE, FLINDERS: Tell el-Hesy (Lachish). Palestine Exploration Fund, 1891.

BLISS, FREDERICK JONES: A Mound of many Cities. Palestine Exploration Fund, 1898.

Tell Zakariya (Azekah)

Tell es-Safi (Gath or Libnah)

Tell el-Judeideh (?)

Tell Sandahannah (Moresheth, Marissa)

BLISS, FREDERICK JONES: Excavations in Palestine during the years 1898–1900. Palestine Exploration Fund, 1902.

PETERS, J. P., and HERMANN THIERSCH: The Marissa Tombs. Palestine Exploration Fund.

Tell Taanach (*Taanach*)

SELLIN (ERNST): Tell Ta'annek, Bericht über eine . . . Ausgrabung in Palästina. Denkschriften der kaiserliche Akademie der Wissenschaften in Wien, vol. 50. Vienna, 1904.

Tell el-Jezari (*Gezer*)

PALESTINE EXPLORATION FUND: Memoir on the Excavation of Gezer. Three vols. Murray, London, 1912.

Tell Mutasellim (*Megiddo*)

SCHUMACHER, G.: Tell el-Mutasellim, Bericht über die 1903 bis 1905 . . . veranstalteten Ausgrabungen. Leipzig, 1908.

Tell es-Sultan (*Jericho*)

SELLIN (ERNST) and CARL WATZINGER: Jericho, die Ergebnisse der Ausgrabungen. Leipzig, 1915.

Ain esh-Shems (*Beth-Shemesh*)

MACKENZIE, DUNCAN: Excavations at Ain Shems (Bethshemesh). Palestine Exploration Fund Annual, vol. 11, 1912–13.

Ashkelon

Reports in Palestine Exploration Fund Quarterly Statement.

Beisan (*Beth-Shean*)

Reports in the *Museum Journal*, University of Pennsylvania.

Sebusteh (*Samaria*)

REISNER (GEORGE ANDREW), CLARENCE STANLEY FISHER, and DAVID GORDON LYON: Harvard Excavations at Samaria, 1908–10. Cambridge (Mass.), 1924.

INDEX

THE END